Yes, We Still Drink Coffee!

A Fighting Words and Front Line Defenders Publication.

Yes, We Still Drink Coffee! is published in June 2019.

FIGHTING WORDS
Behan Square
Russell Street
Dublin 1
D01 WD53
Ireland
www.fightingwords.ie

FRONT LINE DEFENDERS
Second Floor, Grattan House
Temple Road
Blackrock
Co. Dublin
A94 FA39
Ireland
www.frontlinedefenders.org

Printed by:
Walsh Colourprint
Castleisland
Co. Kerry
Ireland

Edited by: Leeann Gallagher
Interior and cover design: Tola Flanagan
Cover artwork: Zehra Doğan

ISBN: 978-0-9935827-5-2

Yes, We Still Drink Coffee!

Stories Of Women Human Rights Defenders

FRONT LINE DEFENDERS

FOREWORD

I had no idea. That was my immediate thought when I first read the essays in this collection. I hadn't realised the price women pay for defending human rights around the world, especially in countries such as Turkey, Somalia, Sudan, Kuwait, Palestine, Egypt and Tunisia.

I should have known, of course. I had read newspaper articles, watched TV reports. I had donated to Amnesty International, signed petitions. I had seen news coverage from troubled countries, heard the sound bites. But too often I'd turned away, thinking it was all happening so far from me, that there was nothing I could do about it, that it was too outside my own experience.

Reading these remarkable essays is a jolt to the conscience. The women interviewed for this collection have chosen activism over apathy. They live with threats and fear, and confront them with courage. They are committed to highlighting injustices, campaigning for change, often at great personal risk.

As a writer, I take everyday freedoms for granted. I can choose my subject matter. I can say what I like on social media. Armed police do not crash through my door at midnight because of my words. I haven't had to endure intimidation, face charges or imprisonment, battle against the noise and terror of war to make my voice heard or get my stories published.

The women featured in this book have faced arrest, prison sentences, threats of rape and death. Some now live in exile from their home countries. Each has a powerful personal story, taking the reader beyond the headlines into their daily lives.

What makes this collection unique is that the women provided their testimonies to a group of women writers. The project has been a collaboration between the Irish creative writing centre Fighting Words and the Dublin-based Front Line Defenders.

Seven Irish-based writers were paired with seven human rights defenders: Laura Cassidy and Lina Ben Mhenni (Tunisia); Catherine Dunne and Hadeel Buqrais (Kuwait); Hilary Fannin and T (Sudan); Lia Mills and Nurcan Baysal (Turkey); Azra Naseem and Muna Hassan (Somalia); Sheila O'Flanagan and Lana Ramadan (Palestine); Melatu Uche Okorie and Seham Osman (Egypt).

There was no formal brief. The writers were simply encouraged to ask questions, to listen, to learn. Some met face-to-face. Others conducted their conversations and interviews entirely by email. There were occasional phone calls. The human rights defenders were also invited to submit essays of their own if they wished, for translation and inclusion.

Each piece took months of negotiation, research, planning. Communication was often difficult, across different territories and time zones. Language was sometimes a barrier, translations time-consuming. Yet each contribution shows the sense of duty and responsibility each woman feels toward the vulnerable and the persecuted.

'We wanted to tell the stories of the women behind the work, bringing their stories to a new and wider audience,' Dr Orla Lehane, education director with Fighting Words, explained. 'The hope is that by sharing the stories in this way more people will become aware of the work of women human rights defenders and recognise the importance of what they do and the difficulties they face.'

The women's personal stories are presented in a variety of ways: in interview form, via direct quotes, in first person, through art and illustration. Two of the human rights defenders – Ezrena Marwan of Malaysia and Zehra Doğan of Turkey – are also talented artists and their work is included. Irish artist Niamh Flanagan's prints accompany Sheila O'Flanagan's story on Lana Ramadan. Irish graphic artist Rosa Devine has interpreted Melatu Uche Okorie's interview with Seham Osman of Egypt. They are all powerful and illuminating examples of storytelling and creativity.

Dr Lehane was heartened by the depth of the goodwill towards the project. 'Witnessing the relationships and conversations between the women human rights defenders and the writers and artists has been really great. The respect the writers have shown for the women they are working with – their desire to work together on the stories, their striving for accuracy within these pieces and ensuring the defenders have final say on the pieces – has been striking.

'In addition to the writers and artists, many people willingly contributed their time to make this collection possible, helping with transcribing interviews, fact-checking stories, translating, interpreting, editing and designing the collection.'

One of the Irish writers, Hilary Fannin, observed, 'I think personal stories and narratives have a chance of breaking through the exhaustion and ennui we experience when it comes to focusing on politics and pain.'

Each of the women interviewed is still campaigning, still taking risks. They are also trying to live full working lives, as well as be daughters, sisters, wives. Those with children combine their activism with the demands of parenting. They all still seek moments of joy, fun and beauty in their lives. They drink coffee, go to the cinema, meet friends, listen to music, make plans. They admit they are tired, sad and fearful at times. They are also courageous. Determined. Optimistic. Their stories can be harrowing, yet they are inspiring.

These women all come from different cultures and speak different languages, but we can immediately empathise with them.

Hilary Fannin profiled T, from Sudan. 'She could be me, or you. Her narrative is ordinary in its extraordinariness. She's the same as us. I was startled by her youth, her vulnerability, her weariness. She seemed – and I repeat the word consciously – entirely ordinary. An ordinary, ethical, sensitive, well-educated young woman, trying to communicate the story of her countrywomen. Her vulnerability was intensely difficult. I feared for her if she was to return to Sudan under Bashir.'

Sheila O'Flanagan wrote about Lana Ramadan of Palestine. 'I loved Lana's sense of family and of shared memories passing through the generations. Even though she's faced very difficult situations, she also comes across as a young, creative woman who enjoys the beautiful things in life, like music and dance, family and friends. She's warm and empathetic and very positive despite her experiences.

'I was very moved by her description of her parents and grandparents and their belief that education was so important for their children. It doesn't matter where you live, the majority of parents think that way. And it reminded me of how all parents, no matter where they are, and no matter what their political beliefs, only want the best for their children.'

Catherine Dunne's essay combines insights into Kuwait's history with the personal story of Hadeel Buqrais. 'Right from the start of the process, what I was most conscious of was my own, mortifying, ignorance. Meeting Hadeel and engaging with the research for the essay was a revelation, and a startling one, about how little of the world I knew. But, in conversation with Hadeel, I became aware in a new and visceral way of a culture and a way of life that I had always regarded as 'other'. Over time, over coffee and emails, over WhatsApp and friendly exchanges, I became aware, more than anything, of the similarities of women's lives everywhere, rather than the differences in culture and religion that might separate us.'

Laura Cassidy has felt a lasting impact from her work with Lina Ben Mhenni of Tunisia. 'I found it devastating to read of all the different ways terrorism had impacted on the people of Tunisia. Lina's positivity and determination continues to be an inspiration for me – we are lucky to have people like her, who dedicate their lives to making their country a better place to live.'

Working on the project and writing about Nurcan Baysal of Turkey reminded Lia Mills 'that we should use our freedoms and democracy consciously and well. We take so much for granted. Stories like these remind us that regimes and tyrants can act with absolute impunity while the world stands by. We think we are safe, here; but how safe are we?'

After reading this collection, perhaps you'll watch the TV news differently, read articles differently. These women's testimonies provide a powerful insight into the reality of defending human rights around the world. Each of the activists has been honest and courageous. The writers have responded with curiosity, empathy and admiration. They are asking us to pay attention. To watch. To listen. To ask ourselves: How can I let this go on? What can I do about it?

It isn't hopeless. We can all do more than turn away, or feel overwhelmed. If we have a platform, we can share their stories, their blogs, their tweets, these essays. Sign petitions. Donate to the organisations on the ground supporting these women and their fellow human rights defenders.

We can all add our voices to their voices.
For their sake, and our sake.

Monica McInerney
May 2019

PREFACE

A small ceramic figure sits on the windowsill in my living room. Affectionately known as 'the scholar' in our house, he has been sitting there, reading his book, since November 2007. November 2007 is when I met Elena Urlaeva, a human rights defender from Uzbekistan. This figurine, wearing traditional Uzbek robes, was Elena's gift to me, carried from Uzbekistan to Dublin.

Elena had travelled to Dublin to participate in the Dublin Platform for Human Rights Defenders, a biennial event organised by Front Line Defenders to bring human rights defenders from almost every country in the world together. It was not an easy trip for Elena. She faced travel restrictions because of her human rights activism.

Leaving Uzbekistan was dangerous for her. Staying in Uzbekistan was also dangerous. In 2001 she was detained and forcibly committed to a psychiatric hospital and repeatedly subjected to months of psychiatric treatment. All because of her human rights work. Elena's story struck me. It has stayed with me. Whatever else comes and goes in our house, Elena's figurine stays.

The stories here, like Elena's, are remarkable. This collection has come about through a partnership between the creative writing centre Fighting Words and the human rights organisation Front Line Defenders. The aim of this collaboration is to bring the stories of women human rights defenders to a new audience, humanising the women behind the work and increasing their visibility.

Fortunate to have worked with both organisations, the similarities underpinning the work of each were clear to me. As this project evolved, this became even clearer. Fighting Words is a creative writing centre established by Roddy Doyle and Seán Love. First opened in Dublin in 2009, and now with locations across the island of Ireland, Fighting Words offers free creative writing programmes and aims to help students of all ages to develop their writing skills and to explore their love of writing. There is always a little bit of magic involved in these workshops. There is a moment when everything clicks. A story comes together. Characters come to life. Words are crossed out, replaced with better words. A throwaway line becomes the hook of a song. And something more is happening. There is a space for voices to be heard and acknowledged. Workshop participants see that their ideas, their stories, their voices matter. They are taken seriously, whether the story is about a time-travelling potato or a pig with dreams of becoming president. They have the freedom to shape their stories as they wish, to have and express ideas, to change their mind and tell their stories in their way.

This freedom of expression is not something to take for granted. It is not something the women featured in this collection can take for granted. In one case, the woman remains anonymous. Sharing her identity is simply too dangerous.

Front Line Defenders was founded in Dublin in 2001, with the specific aim of protecting human rights defenders at risk. These are individuals around the world who work, non-violently and often in very dangerous situations, for any or all of the rights enshrined in the Universal Declaration of Human Rights. In addition to practical supports to address the protection needs identified by human rights defenders themselves, Front Line creates opportunities and events for human rights defenders to come together to network, share their stories and support one another, while raising awareness of the issues with which they are faced.

Having attended such events, and heard these stories and testimonies, it became clear that these stories are important. They need to be told. They need to be heard. This collection highlights the importance of story and of freedom of expression. Central to this work is the belief that everyone has a story to tell, and sharing these stories can help us to understand our varied lives.

It has taken a long time to put this collection of stories together. Honouring these women and getting their stories right has been important to all the writers and artists. In addition to arranging times to meet, and the lengthy travel that made these meetings possible, this has involved many follow-up phone calls, emails and text conversations. It has involved research on the part of the writers. They wanted to get the details right, to understand something of the complex situations in which these women work. In some cases, they were working across languages. The women human rights defenders all had the final say on the works included here. They patiently fielded these phone calls and questions, all the while leading busy lives, getting on with their work.

Working together has provided a special opportunity for these women human rights defenders to partner with writers and artists to create this anthology of work. Thank you to these amazing women for taking the time to share their important stories. Thanks also to the writers and artists who worked with them to bring these stories to our readers. Finally, thanks to everyone who contributed their skills and expertise to this publication.

Dr Orla Lehane
Education Director, Fighting Words
May 2019

ACKNOWLEDGEMENTS

Our thanks first and foremost to the women human rights defenders who shared their powerful stories with us. Thank you to the writers and artists who worked with these women to bring their work to our readers. In addition, we would like to thank all of those who generously contributed their time and skills to help make this publication possible:

Andrew Anderson, *Banshee Literary Journal*, Sara Bennett, Dr Erika Biagini, Ellie Buckhout, Ozlem Dalkiran, Moataz El Fegiery, Tanya Farrelly, Lauren Foley, Michelle Foley, Freedom to Write Campaign (Ireland), Lisa Harding, Julie Kavanagh, Dr Ian Kelly, Erin Kilbride, Dr Walt Kilroy, Mary Lawlor, Ray Lynn, Peter McCloskey, Maria McManus, Tara Madden, Khouloud Nsiri, Naz Oke, Ivi Oliveira, Jef Rabillion, Staccato Literary Salon, Adam Shapiro, Emmeline Suddock, Fiona Wong.

CONTRIBUTING ARTISTS

Zehra Doğan
   pp: cover, inside cover, 8, 55, 60, 83
   Artwork photographed by Jef Rabillion

Ezrena Marwan
   pp: facing 1, 29, 67, 73, 93
   Originally created as part of the 'Apa Kata'
   Exhibition, a collaboration between the Malaysian
   Design Archive and Sisters in Islam:
   http://www.sejarahwanita.org/apa-kata/

Niamh Flanagan
   pp: 20 – *The Lost Villages*
   pp: 23 – *The Past Seeps Up from Under*

Rosa Devine
   pp: 40 – 48

CONTENTS

YES, WE STILL DRINK COFFEE!

written by **Nurcan Baysal**

I grew up in one of the poor districts of Diyarbakır, the biggest city in Turkey's mainly Kurdish south-east. At the beginning of the 1980s, we began to hear that there was some kind of armed conflict in the mountains, between 'terrorists' and the state. After a while, we heard these 'terrorists' were called 'Apocu'. They were Kurdish and fighting for the rights of Kurdish people. Many Kurdish people still had no idea about the PKK, the Kurdistan Workers' Party, as the Apocu were formally known.

In the 1980s, there were a lot of tears, a lot of sadness and a lot of funerals in my small neighbourhood. Children were leaving and their dead bodies were returning. Most of the suffering was in silence. People were afraid. After so many years, ordinary people did not have an understanding of what it meant to suffer for the Kurdish cause.

In the beginning of the 1990s, everyone was aware of the war in the mountains. We learned about the PKK. Every day the TV showed the PKK. Yet we knew the people they said were 'terrorists' were none other than our brothers and sisters, our neighbours, and our uncles.

I remember older students at school collected history books and burnt them in the schoolyard. They told us these history books did not include us, the Kurdish people. 'This is not our history. Burn them!' they said.

After the local head of the Kurdish party HEP [People's Labour Party], Vedat Aydın, was murdered by the state on 10 July 1991, hundreds of thousands of people gathered for his funeral in Diyarbakır. The security forces, with their Kalashnikovs in hand, fired into the crowd. Dozens were killed. We still do not know exactly how many people died that day. But after that thousands of young Kurds went to the mountains to join the PKK.

During the 1990s, the silence of the 1980s turned to protest. Thousands began to participate in the funerals of young people coming back from the mountains. Parents proudly declared their children had died for the rights of Kurdish people. Festivities to mark the Kurdish new year – Newroz – became a place where Kurdish people defied the state, showing themselves, their demands and their power.

During those years, there were bombings, killings and forced disappearances in city centres, but until 2015 active combat between the state and PKK was mainly confined to the mountains.

In 2015, the war came to our city centres. Heavy clashes between the youth wing of the PKK and the state began. Military curfews were declared in city centres. The historical centre of Diyarbakır, Sur, was under heavy bombardment by the state for one hundred days. Thousands of people who lived in Sur were trapped in their houses.

During the bombardment, many people from outside the Kurdish region criticised the people of Diyarbakır for sitting in coffee houses.

Even democrats, journalists and writers who came to visit the city for only a few days reported that life continued outside of Sur, and that the people of Diyarbakır were indifferent to their suffering. 'While Sur is under bombardment, they drink coffee. What kind of people are they?' they asked.

They have no idea what it is like to live in war. Life continues even in war. When a bomb drops, life stops for a minute, but then it continues. Children go to school, parents go to work, the sick are taken to hospitals, we drink coffee and sometimes we even make jokes under bombardment, through tear gas and during protests. War is a part of our life. We know that we are mortal, and this feeling accompanies you all the time.

I remember one of my friends took her little son to the cinema one day during the bombardment. She told me: 'The sound of the bombs never stops. We were inside the house for weeks. My son was getting worse. He thought that he would die. With each bomb, he jumped under the dinner table and screamed, "Mom, I died." I thought it might be better to go outside; maybe this would help my children. I took them to the cinema. While we were watching the film, I thought how nice it was not to hear the sound of bombs for a few hours. Then I began to cry, I am such a bad person. Now, outside, bombs are dropping and people are dying and I am watching a film in the cinema! I was ashamed.'

Every day, outside Sur, a few people were killed at protests for those under bombardment. Tear gas hung over the city. And still life continued under the sounds of bombs, guns and armoured vehicles, together creating an inescapable sound: the sound of death.

Today, there are no bombs dropping on the city centres. But there is heavy state pressure, thousands of people are in prison, arrests continue and people live in fear. There is silence again. People outside the region are now criticising this silence.

There are many reasons for this silence: the pressure of the state, witnessing such extreme cruelty and young people being killed so easily. Although there is silence, people are struggling.

Many NGOs were closed. Some of them opened again in silence. People continue their work and support each other in silence. The struggle does not always have to be on the street. When you re-open an NGO, this is a struggle. When you continue to write, this is a struggle. The river of freedom flows. Maybe not wildly at the moment, but it flows.

Amidst all this cruelty, we are the people who refuse to leave this land, who are still here and still struggling. And yes, we still drink coffee!

This piece was first published on Ahval News on 18 April 2018.
www.ahvalnews.com

HADEEL BUQRAIS (Kuwait)
written by Catherine Dunne

Hadeel Buqrais is an active human rights defender and writer in her native Kuwait. She works as a freelancer to monitor and document human rights violations by the Kuwaiti government. She previously worked for Kuwait Watch, an NGO that works on the development of legal protections for people in her native country.

*

When Hadeel and I meet, she is still astonished by what she'd noticed in her walks around Dublin the previous day. She has never been to Ireland before. That's where our conversation begins: her initial impressions of her first time outside Kuwait.

We sit in the corner of a hotel restaurant, hoping for quiet. It's early morning. The staff clatter around us, busying themselves with cleaning, laying tables, vacuum-cleaning. Hadeel is soft-spoken and we lean towards each other so that we can hear more easily. Her expression is animated as she recounts the number of charity shops she remembers spotting in the city centre the day before.

'All of them', she says, 'that are there only to help others? Can this be true? Shops for those with cancer, help for the blind, help for children: this is not something I have ever seen before. And free legal aid!'

I am tempted to suggest that there might be another interpretation: that perhaps the presence of so many charity shops says as much about the poor funding of essential services as it does about the generosity of Irish people, but for now, I don't. I want to hear what she has to say.

She tells me that Kuwait is 'a very materialistic society'. Conspicuous consumption is the fashion there. Such excess makes Hadeel feel uncomfortable. It goes against her personal moral system. It is anathema to the teachings of Islam.

Hadeel believes that it is government policy to encourage people's consumerism. 'It stops the population from becoming political,' she says. 'Material things become a kind of displacement activity. It's like: "We have money, we shop."'

It's how Kuwaiti people 'like to define themselves', their place in the world. 'We have wealth, so much wealth. And a highly educated population,' Hadeel shakes her head. 'We have no need to treat our minorities so badly.'

*

Kuwait is a small emirate positioned between two very large and powerful neighbours, Iraq and Saudi Arabia. This country of some 18,000 square kilometres lies in one of the driest, most inhospitable deserts on earth. It is, however, strategically positioned on the Persian Gulf.

It was here, on the shores of Kuwait Bay, that in the eighteenth century, Bedouin from the interior founded a trading post. The name 'Kuwait' has its origin in the Arabic diminutive of the Hindustani word kūt ('fort').

Kuwait's ruling family, the Āl Ṣabāḥ, formally established a sheikhdom there in 1756. Since then, the country's wealth has always been linked with foreign commerce. Over time, this small fort grew to become Kuwait City, now home to the vast majority of the country's population of some 4.1 million. Kuwait City is filled with skyscrapers, modern apartment buildings, mosques and carefully planned suburban developments.

Given Kuwait's strategic location on the Persian Gulf, Britain's East India Company (EIC) saw its massive potential as a trade route back in the nineteenth century. Kuwait happened to lie between that company's primary centre of production, India, and its most important markets, the United Kingdom and Europe. In addition, Kuwait possessed a deep-water port, one of the best in the Northern Gulf. This meant it could easily accommodate British ships, making it an attractive proposition for the loading and unloading of cargo, and also for passenger ships to dock.

In the late nineteenth century, Kuwait was becoming increasingly keen to foster a closer relationship with Britain, particularly as it was anxious to move away from the influence of Ottoman rule. In 1899, it became a British protectorate. This was a relationship that would continue for more than sixty years.

However, in 1961, when Kuwait had severed its formal ties with Britain – by all accounts, an amicable separation – a new revolutionary government in Iraq claimed Kuwait as part of Iraqi territory. This was not the first time that Iraq had claimed ownership of Kuwait. The first claim had surfaced back in 1938, the year oil was first discovered in the emirate. Neither Iraq nor the Ottoman Empire had ever formally ruled Kuwait, but Iraq continued to assert a vague title to the land, a claim obscured by the mists of history.

Under General Abdul Karim Kassem in June 1961, Iraqi tanks and soldiers advanced towards the sheikhdom. Kuwait's ruler, Sheikh Abdullah, made appeals to other Arab states for help, but his calls fell on deaf ears and he was forced to rely upon his defence agreement with Britain. British forces landed in July of that same year to let General Kassem know, in no uncertain terms, that Kuwait and British oil were not for the taking. Close economic and strategic links between Britain and Kuwait have been maintained right up until the present day.

Kuwait drew world attention in 1990 when Iraqi forces once again invaded and attempted to annex the emirate. A United Nations coalition, led by the US, drove Iraq's army out of Kuwait in February 1991, some seven months after the invasion. Iraqi forces looted the country as they retreated and set fire to more than seven hundred of Kuwait's nine hundred and fifty oil wells. The fires consumed more than six million barrels of oil per day. But by the autumn of 1991, all the fires had been extinguished and production quickly got back to normal.

Sara Akbar was Kuwait's first female petroleum engineer in the field. During the Iraqi invasion, she led a group of oil employees to maintain machinery and ensure the supply of electricity. After the retreating Iraqi troops set the oil fields on fire, Akbar set up a specialist team to control and extinguish the fires. She earned herself the nickname 'Firefighter'.

*

Hadeel was eleven years old when Iraq invaded her homeland. 'I grew up understanding that Iraq had always claimed ownership of Kuwait,' she says. 'That they believed our land was theirs from the beginning; that there was no such thing as Kuwait. So there was always fear: the little neighbour's fear of the big neighbour devouring it.'

At about 2 a.m. local time on 2 August 1990, the Iraqi army quickly overwhelmed Kuwait's defence forces. Those who remained retreated to Saudi Arabia. The emir of Kuwait, Sheikh Sabah Al Ahmad Al Jabir Al Sabah, his family, and other government leaders fled to Saudi Arabia, and within hours the Iraqis had set up a provincial government. By annexing Kuwait, Iraq gained control of twenty per cent of the world's oil reserves. It also took control of a substantial part of the coastline on the Persian Gulf.

The same day, the United Nations Security Council condemned the invasion and demanded Iraq's immediate withdrawal from Kuwait. But it would take the coalition forces of Operation Desert Storm another seven months of fighting before Iraq was finally defeated. It's impossible to verify the number of civilian casualties suffered by Kuwait and Iraq during this horrific seven months – estimates vary from one hundred thousand to two hundred thousand – before the ceasefire was declared on 28 February 1991.

It is also reported that over two hundred thousand Palestinians fled the country during the Iraqi invasion, fearing for their safety and their lives. During that time, Kuwaiti anger at Palestine was intense; they bitterly opposed the alignment of Yasser Arafat and the Palestine Liberation Organisation (PLO) with Saddam Hussein. As a result, Palestinians resident in Kuwait were both harassed and intimidated by Iraqi forces, as well as suddenly finding themselves fired from their Kuwaiti employment. Along with other civilians, they suffered chronic food shortages and a lack of proper medical care. And similar to the fate of those Kuwaitis who fled the Iraqi invasion, Palestinians who had been living and working peacefully in Kuwait – the vast majority of teachers in girls' schools there, for example, were Palestinian women – were made penniless as a result of the war. Most of the two hundred thousand who fled made their way to Jordan as refugees, in search of a new life.

*

Hadeel still remembers how, during that turbulent time, her mother would not give her eleven-year-old daughter permission to protest against the Iraqi invasion. She remembers how powerless she felt at that, how badly she 'wanted to do the right thing', even as a young child. So, rather than take to the streets, as she wanted to, Hadeel made a puppet theatre, as a way of keeping herself and the other children occupied. She also made sure to help her elderly neighbours to access water.

She has no difficulty recalling the national sense of shock at the invasion, the all-pervasive feeling of high alert, of needing 'to look over your shoulder the whole time'. She remembers the constant adult conversations in which everyone worried about their immediate future – 'What is next?' 'Who is next?' She remembers also how the narrative went afterwards; how, once the war was over, Kuwaiti citizens were required to be grateful to Saudi Arabia and the United States. Together, they had saved the Kuwaiti nation. Together, they had liberated the country from the old enemy, Iraq.

*

Hadeel tells me about the first time she felt impelled to go to the defence of another. At school, as a young girl, she saw one of her schoolmates being attacked. He was younger than she was, taunted and bullied because of his colour. She threw herself into the fray and used her own body as a shield to protect him.

Afterwards, she was heavily criticised for behaving immodestly. Her actions were not those of a 'proper girl'. There were very strict rules for how girls should conduct themselves, she recalls, and they were very different from the rules that governed the boys. But she became conscious of a powerful need as a result of that experience. She knew she had the instinct to 'protect the underdog'.

Hadeel comes from a wealthy, privileged and very religious Sunni Muslim background. Her family has always resisted her efforts to become involved in defending the human rights of others. She understands their fears, she says. In Kuwait, human rights activism can be seen as criminal activity and attracts severe penalties. Any kind of protest is seen as 'anti-patriotic'. Nonetheless, Hadeel persevered, and consciously educated herself throughout her adolescence and early adulthood by reading everything she could get her hands on that related to the defence of human rights.

In 2011, despite family opposition, she travelled to Lebanon to attend a training course aimed at supporting and educating human rights defenders. Once again, it was a personal experience that drove her instinct to learn more.

She'd had a friend, Fatma, who suffered from sickle-cell anaemia and was being treated in Bahrain, at the Salmaniya hospital. A state of emergency had been declared in Bahrain at that time, in 2011. The Salmaniya had come under attack by Saudi forces, and in the ensuing chaos, Fatma died. Hadeel saw how all attempts afterwards to tell the truth about the attack failed. She believes that the media are frequently 'in Saudi ownership, or owned by those sympathetic to Saudi Arabia. They never tell the truth.'

*

Kuwait is a member of the Gulf Cooperation Council (GCC), a political and economic alliance of six Middle Eastern countries, along with Saudi Arabia, the United Arab Emirates (UAE), Qatar, Bahrain, and

Oman. Established in Abu Dhabi in 1981, the GCC was originally formed to foster closer ties among the energy-rich Gulf states. Its founding charter emphasised issues of social and cultural cohesion, along with environmental and scientific cooperation, but to Western eyes, the alliance also had a great deal to do with internal security.

The GCC countries tend to have young and rapidly expanding populations – although the rate of growth differs from country to country. All of the states rely on the communities of expatriate workers that have grown exponentially in recent decades, in tandem with the expanding economies. Estimates from 2010–13 show that in Saudi Arabia, expatriate workers made up thirty-two per cent (9.2 million) of the population. In the UAE, the figure was eighty-nine per cent (7.3 million) expats. Qatar had eighty-seven per cent (1.7 million) expatriate workers and in Bahrain the figure was fifty-nine per cent (7.3 million). Oman had forty-four per cent (1.6 million), and finally, in Kuwait, the numbers of expatriate workers reached seventy per cent of the population, or 2.65 million people. The imbalance between national and foreign populations has resulted in internal tensions in many GCC countries.

Those non-Kuwaiti nationals working in Kuwait, for example, do not enjoy citizenship rights, economic or political, which are designed exclusively for Kuwaiti citizens. To be defined as a citizen, one must be able to prove Kuwaiti ancestry prior to 1920. Naturalisation is strictly limited. Kuwaiti citizens are almost entirely Muslim, and a law passed in 1981 limits citizenship to Muslims. The majority are Sunni but about one-third are Shī'ite and while tension in Kuwait has largely focused on migrant workers, there is also an uneasy relationship between the Sunni and the Shī'ite, as the latters' loyalties are seen to lie with Iran.

*

Hadeel and I discuss the plight of the migrant workers who come to Kuwait from all over India, Bangladesh and Pakistan. They are trapped once they arrive, according to Hadeel, in a kind of 'modern slavery'.

Migrants must pay anything from 1,000–2,000 Kuwaiti Dinars[i] (€3,000–€6,000) for permission to work in Kuwait. After that, there is a further 700 KD (€2,100) due in order to secure employment. Many unskilled labourers will receive around 25 KD (€75) per month, whereas the top rate for those who are highly skilled averages 700 KD (€2,100).

Human Rights Watch's *World Report 2019: Events of 2018* states:

> In 2015, Kuwait issued a new standard contract for migrant workers, and a 2016 administrative decision allowed some migrant workers to transfer their sponsorship to a new employer after three years of work, without their employer's consent. However, these reforms do not include migrant domestic workers.

> In 2015, the National Assembly passed a law granting domestic workers the right to a weekly day off, 30 days of annual paid leave, a 12-hour working day with rest, and an end-of-service benefit of one

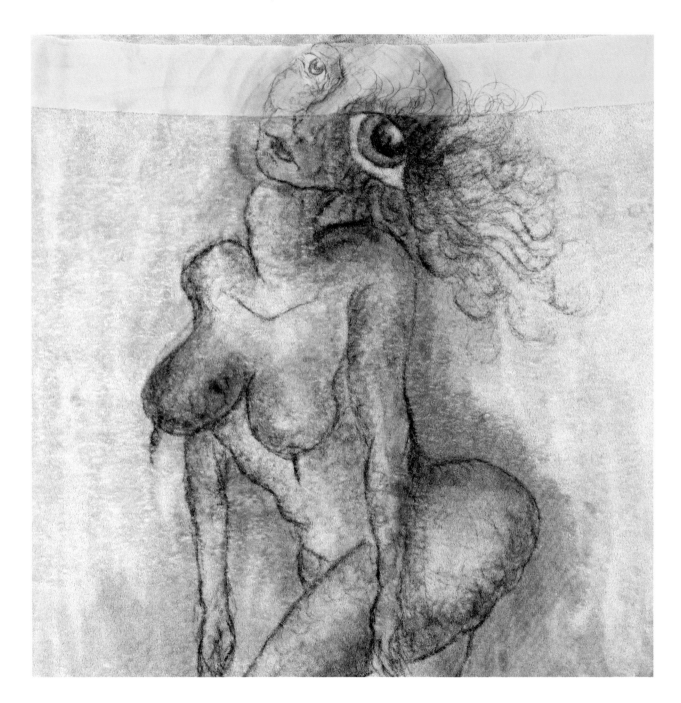

month a year at the end of the contract, among other rights. In 2016 and 2017, the Interior Ministry passed implementing regulations for the law, and mandated that employers must pay overtime compensation. The ministry also issued a decree establishing a minimum wage of KD 60 (US $200) for domestic workers.[ii]

Nearly ninety per cent of all Kuwaiti households employ a foreign domestic worker. However, the law is weak and lacks consistent enforcement: it 'does not set out sanctions against employers who confiscate passports or fail to provide adequate housing, food, and medical expenses, work breaks, or weekly rest days'.[iii]

Hadeel has little confidence in the efficacy of current labour laws where migrant workers are concerned. 'Employers routinely confiscate the passports of their employees,' she says. 'If you don't like it, you can always leave' is the prevailing attitude, and 'it's immoral. Pay to be enslaved.' She says that the Indian government has a duty to protect its citizens, but it is a duty that is largely ignored and discrimination is widespread.

Official India is 'very careful to maintain its relationship with Kuwait. If problems arise, everyone agrees that the Indian, or Pakistani, or Bangladeshi worker is the problem. Never the Kuwaiti employer.'

Within the more lucrative oil industry, migrant workers frequently lose their jobs on a trumped-up charge, particularly if they are 'troublesome'. Wealthy Kuwaitis often have family members 'waiting in the wings', Hadeel says, especially for the better-paying jobs. 'As soon as the family member is free to take up employment, the migrant worker is fired. And there are no pro bono human rights lawyers in Kuwait to take up their case. That mentality does not exist. Lawyers will only work if you pay them. So the migrant worker has no access to a proper legal defence.'

'These workers will eat us,' the popular slogan goes. 'They will eat our jobs. They will eat everything.' Hadeel rejects this. 'Nobody is going to eat anything,' she says. 'That is not a well-founded fear. Those complaints are simply racism in another form.'

Most of the large employers in Kuwait are tied to the hugely wealthy oil industry. And the oil companies are overwhelmingly owned and run by a group of powerful Kuwaiti families.

'Oil companies pay very well,' Hadeel says, and now they are coming 'under increasing pressure by the Kuwaiti government not to employ foreigners in the higher-level jobs'. To employ expats for more menial work is fine, as native Kuwaitis don't want to do the menial jobs themselves. 'During the Iraqi invasion,' Hadeel says, 'everyone worked at everything. But not any longer.'

*

Kuwait has now, by and large, recovered from the effects of the war of 1990–1. It has, once again, one of the highest per capita incomes in the world. Its government continues to be conservative and no criticism of the emir is tolerated. Powerful elements in society have resisted social reforms such as women's suffrage, and women had no right to vote until 2005. Women voted for the first time in the elections of June 2006. Out of 250 candidates, 28 were women. None was elected. Four years later, four women were elected to parliament for the first time. Nonetheless, in 2011, Kuwait was ranked highest of all the Arab countries in gender equality, in the Human Development Report's Gender Equality Index.

*

In April 2017, Hadeel felt the time was right to make the fight for women's rights more visible. She spearheaded an event called 'Namshi Laha' or 'Walking for Her'. This was an hour-long protest, a defiant walk through the streets of the capital, Kuwait City, in solidarity with the women of Saudi Arabia, who were demanding gender equality.

The 2011–14 campaign in Saudi Arabia, where women fought for permission to drive, caused a huge backlash. A spokesman for the government warned that 'women in Saudi are banned from driving and laws will be applied against violators and those who demonstrate support'.[iv] The campaign was eventually successful, but, as of August 2018, some twelve women activists were still detained in prison in Saudi Arabia.

During the Namshi Laha campaign in Kuwait, the women who took part wore pink ribbons as a symbol of support for their Saudi sisters. As a result of that hour-long, peaceful demonstration through the streets of the city, Hadeel became the target of vile abuse on social media. 'They called me "whore" and "traitor",' she says. 'They threatened me and my family.'

The conservative Waleed Al-Tabtabaie, a member of the Kuwaiti National Assembly, and a man who is intensely loyal to the regime in Saudi, made political capital out of the march, claiming that it had been staged by Iran. He condemned Hadeel's active participation and said she was nothing better than 'an ambassador for Iran'. It was an accusation, she says, that was completely without foundation. Nonetheless, in the aftermath of the march, Hadeel was subjected to numerous threats to her personal safety: serious threats to rape her, kill her, and harm her children.

'It was a terrifying time,' she says, and she had to suspend her human rights activities for a full six months until the furore had died down. During that time, she kept her two children close to home and lived with the constant expectation of random attacks on her and her family.

Hadeel is convinced that the Kuwaiti government colluded in the campaign of vilification against her. 'They used my divorce against me. They made information about my children public. They made it clear that no criticism of Saudi would be tolerated. It was like a social death penalty,' she says, as she lived in increasing isolation. 'We are not permitted to say anything negative about our "big sister", Saudi Arabia. It, after all, is the perfect representation of the "real Islam". Since then, I do not feel safe in my own country.'

*

The recent murder of the journalist, Jamal Khashoggi in Istanbul, has shone an international spotlight on the evils of the ultra-conservative regime in Saudi. Its repressive activities are very familiar to Hadeel. From the sentencing of three lawyers in 2014 – each of whom received eight years in prison for tweeting criticisms of the Ministry for Justice – to the frequent harassment and intimidation of women seeking gender equality, to the ill-treatment of migrant workers, to the imprisonment and torture of journalists and human rights activists, and to current accusations of war crimes in Yemen, where Saudi-led air strikes seek to secure the return to power of the Sunni leader, Mansur Hadi, Saudi's extremely repressive regime is a constant presence in the air of Kuwait, an all-pervasive threat by the infinitely more powerful 'big sister'.

Hadeel claims that since the 1960s, a large number of Saudi citizens have been granted Kuwaiti citizenship. The Kuwaiti government granted such citizenship rights in an effort to ensure that the Sunnis were the majority population in Kuwait; a move no doubt motivated by the suspicion that Shias will always, first and foremost, be loyal to Iran.

There are also Saudi banks in Kuwait, Hadeel says. An Islamic bank, Bank al Tamweel, which is bound by strict religious laws governing financial transactions, is long established in her country. The 1970s and 1980s saw the rise of Islamic banking across all of the GCC countries. Similarly strict banking regulations exist throughout the entire region.

There is also, she claims, Saudi control of the mass media. 'We have to be careful. We have nothing to protect us against them.'

Hadeel regards some of the more recent social changes in Saudi Arabia as 'cosmetic'. 'The regime is trying to establish a better surface,' she says, 'by doing things like allowing women to drive. But nothing fundamental has changed.'

Hadeel reveals that she, along with many other Kuwaitis, has friends who have been imprisoned in Saudi jails for some perceived slight. 'We don't know where any of them are,' she says. 'All we know is that Saudi jails are appalling. They are like a public toilet. And prisoners there have no rights. There are no laws to protect them.'

And to speak out against your 'big sister' is to invite an immediate response from the Kuwaiti authorities, certain intimidation and a possible prison sentence. Hadeel also fears that her ex-husband – a government official, working in the Kuwaiti Ministry for Defence – will use her human rights activities to take their children away from her.

'They are only young,' she says, 'eleven and twelve years old. They don't know enough to be terrified. And they support, as best they can, the work I do for protecting human rights.' They want to do the right thing, she says, but Hadeel's own mother uses the children to pressurise her into stopping her activities. 'When my children witness these fights,' she says, 'then they become frightened.'

Hadeel worries about her children, constantly. There is a constant tension between her commitment to her human rights activism, and her love and concern for her two children.

'It is very hard,' she says, 'to be a good parent and a human rights defender.'

*

The status of women in Kuwait continues to be a very difficult area to navigate. 'Our position as women is weak,' Hadeel says. 'There is discrimination against us in all areas of our lives.' She notes the fact that the Kuwaiti government provides low-cost, subsidised housing of good quality for Kuwaiti citizens who happen to be male. Similar housing is not available to women. Housing that is made available to women is often of a much poorer quality and located in isolated areas where women do not feel safe.

Divorced women are frequently the targets of sexual harassment. Their status in society is automatically reduced once they no longer have the official protection of a man. After their divorces become final, women will usually return with their children to their own original family homes, Hadeel says. 'That way, if they remarry, custody of the children will not revert to the ex-husband. Instead, the grandmother acquires custody. In that way, the divorced woman will not lose her children.' Furthermore, if a Kuwaiti woman marries a non-Kuwaiti national, she cannot pass on her nationality to her children.

And while divorce is available for both women and men, it is the woman who must apply to the courts for a divorce, and even then, she is permitted only limited grounds of appeal. Men, however, are permitted to unilaterally divorce their wives.

Men can take up to four wives, without the permission or knowledge of any of the women concerned. A man can also prohibit his wife from working if he deems her career to negatively affect the family's interests.

Kuwait has no laws prohibiting domestic violence or marital rape. In 2015, a law that established family courts also set up a centre to deal with cases of domestic violence; however, the centre is obliged to prioritise reconciliation over protection for domestic violence survivors.

> Article 153 of the Kuwaiti penal code stipulates that a man who finds his mother, wife, sister or daughter in the act of adultery and kills them is punished by either a small fine or no more than three years in prison.[v]

Adultery and extramarital intercourse are criminalised, and same-sex relations between men are punishable by up to seven years in prison. In 2017, Kuwait reportedly deported seventy-six men on suspicion of being gay. Transgender people can be arrested under a 2007 penal code provision that prohibits 'imitating the opposite sex in any way'.

*

The abuse by phone, email, text and on social media after the Namshi Laha campaign in 2017 has had a profound and lasting effect on Hadeel. I ask her how she manages to live under such intense pressure. She has an unvarying daily routine, she tells me, which helps her to structure a certain amount of normality into her life.

'I get up before sunrise,' she says. 'That is my time for prayer, before the sun comes up.' Her faith is very important to her. 'It heals me from the inside,' she says. 'It is my moral compass. My faith pervades everything that I do.'

But she never forces Islam on others. 'I love my faith,' she says, 'and I understand that other people love their faith, too. I respect other religions. Faith is not about compulsion.' She is interested in how other people worship their own God, 'It is something we all have in common. I celebrate the Christian faith also, and the Bahá'í. What I hate above all is hypocrisy.'

Hadeel works as a receptionist during the week. She is employed by the Ministry for the Interior. 'I am a perfectionist,' she says. 'I take pride in my work and I make sure to concentrate fully for the seven hours of each day that I am behind the desk.'

Her children come home from school at 1.30 p.m. There are the normal homework activities to be supervised, all the ordinary daily domestic tasks to be completed and Hadeel believes in a strict bedtime routine. 'The afternoons are busy', she says, 'and that time with the children keeps me grounded. I never have any time for myself. It feels strange to have some now, during these days [in Dublin].'

She recalls how the company of her children helped her to survive the campaign of psychological warfare that erupted after Namshi Laha. 'I tried not to show it, but I was completely terrified,' she says. 'I shook constantly. I vomited over and over again in response to all that hatred. I had to shower three times a day because I was sweating profusely. And my family exerted huge pressure on me to cease my activities. They were ashamed of me. They wanted nothing to do with anything I was involved in.'

Some time spent in Lebanon helped. Organisations there such as Amnesty International, Human Rights Watch and the OHCHR (Office of the High Commissioner for Human Rights) helped Hadeel's human rights activism in every way possible. She says that Lebanese society in general has always been a very vibrant supporter of the struggle, that she has felt cherished and her work validated in so many ways. With such practical and emotional support, and with her own 'combination of prayer, yoga and writing, [she] was able to cope'.

Hadeel is a prizewinning writer. One of her poems, 'Fabric', explores transformative experiences in the lives of women. She uses the metaphor of three different textiles to represent the 'rites of passage in a woman's life: marriage, birth and death'. She uses her writing to highlight how women are perceived by Kuwaiti society. She loves the use of symbolic language. One of her plays, 'Our Living Box', explores the gulf of misunderstanding between men and women, each of them inhabiting a separate universe whose walls are impenetrable by the other. She has also written a screenplay that explores the revolution in Bahrain from the perspective of a young Kuwaiti woman.

'Writing', she says, 'saves me. It becomes my sanity.'

*

Amnesty International, in its report on 'Kuwait 2017/18', observed the following:

> The authorities continued to unduly restrict freedom of expression, including by prosecuting and imprisoning government critics and banning certain publications. Members of the Bidun minority continued to face discrimination and were denied citizenship rights. Migrant workers remained inadequately protected against exploitation and abuse. Courts continued to hand down death sentences and executions resumed after a hiatus of four years.[vi]

'Bidun' – the word in Arabic, literally translated, means 'nothing', or 'without nationality'. Though they are classified as a 'stateless people', many of the GCC countries nevertheless treat the Bidun as illegal immigrants. They claim that the Bidun routinely destroy their documents of identification so that they can live and work in the country of their choice. As such, they are discriminated against in every aspect of their lives: work, healthcare and education.

In excess of four thousand Bidun children are denied access to education in Kuwait, by the simple expedient of refusing to issue them with identity cards. The card is essential, Hadeel says, to access anything in Kuwait, from education to healthcare. 'The children don't exist', she says, 'without an ID. And nobody can go to school without an ID, so the policy is to deny the existence of Bidun children.'

Because the Bidun come from the 'northern tribes' of Iraq and Syria, and are neither of Saudi or Kuwaiti descent, they are a completely marginalised community. They also belong to the Shia sect, and this adds further fuel to the fire. 'If the Shia grow to outnumber us, then we will belong to Iran' is a commonly held belief in Kuwait. 'If you give nationality to a Shia, then you make a citizen of someone who is loyal to Iran, not to Kuwait,' Hadeel says. 'This is the fiction that people believe.'

But Hadeel says that there is currently a growing awareness among the Bidun that there are certain rights in existence to which they are entitled. Although Kuwait never signed the International Convention of Human Rights, there are several NGOs at work in Kuwait today. 'Their emphasis on human rights generally has helped the Bidun to speak out without fear. There is global interest in their situation. And pressure is building both from outside and inside Kuwait to focus on their plight.'

To add to the complicated mix of racial and religious intolerance towards the Bidun, there is also the problem of Kuwait's relationship with the other GCC countries, and particularly, as we have seen, with the 'big sister', Saudi.

But all the existing alliances are coming under strain, Hadeel believes. Bahrain – another 'little sister' – is putting pressure on Kuwait not to rock the boat, not to do anything to fracture the relationship with the other 'little sisters'.

It's a tricky balance to maintain, but Kuwait is 'managing relationships very cleverly', Hadeel says, with 'a lot of political manoeuvring'. She says such high maintenance is necessary: Kuwait feels 'surrounded – and not just geographically'. There is an acute awareness in the country of the might of Iraq, Iran and Saudi Arabia. Kuwait needs to tread carefully.

*

In November 2017, Hadeel focused all of her attention on establishing her own school: somewhere that would give her a base from which to build public awareness of the need to protect human rights. Mindful of, but undeterred by, the threats to which she had been subjected after the Namshi Laha campaign, Hadeel set about engaging in the practical activity of educating others – initially children, but also adults – so that they would be equipped to take part in the fight for equality.

She found the right place for a classroom. She bought the tables and chairs herself. She developed the curriculum personally and began to teach others about the concepts of equality and tolerance. It is important that 'human rights' be seen not as a theory, she believes, but as something that applied to everybody's everyday life, all the time.

By the end of 2017, Hadeel had trained almost a hundred volunteers in the area of human rights awareness. She was supported in this work, she says, by Lebanon, most specifically by the Lebanese branch of the Amnesty Human Rights Academy.

Classes can last either a day or a week, and certificates are awarded to each participant. Hadeel taught her students how to post safely on social media, without subjecting themselves to the danger of being indicted for 'technical and digital crimes'. During two-day workshops, she continues to teach participants how to avoid danger areas – they must never use words such as 'Yemen', she says, or 'war'. The cautious wording of tweets and other postings on social media means awareness of human rights abuses can be successfully disseminated – but carefully, always carefully. 'I want to keep everyone out of jail,' Hadeel says. The school is 'slowly growing in acceptance'.

But perhaps her greatest work at the moment is her campaign for the children of the Bidun. 'They have a natural right to go to school,' she says. 'Education is one of their fundamental human rights.'

Hadeel has embarked upon the fight to enable access to school for these stateless children. She also set up an online funding campaign and her aim is to provide every Bidun child with a schoolbag. 'It's an important symbol for them,' she says. The schoolbags are brightly coloured, instantly identifiable as such, and the children are proud to carry them. The Schoolbag Campaign has been active since 2012.

She works in cooperation with schools to provide scholarships for Bidun children – one way of helping them access education when they don't have the all-important identity card.

About eighty per cent of the population of Kuwait is literate. General education is compulsory for native Kuwaitis between the ages of six and fourteen. It is entirely free, part of Kuwait's cradle-to-grave welfare state, and also includes school meals, books, uniforms, transportation and medical attention. Non-Kuwaiti students typically attend private schools.

'It's extraordinary,' she says. 'My country is a very generous donor to educational campaigns in Africa, for example. But at home, for the Bidun, it's a very different story.'

But individuals are continuing to donate: 50 KD (€150) is enough to send a child to school, and the campaign is constantly gathering momentum. 'Things have to change,' she says. 'The level of discrimination against the Bidun is incredible. They cannot have a bank account, for example. The suicide rates in the community are huge. Just last year, two teenagers set themselves on fire in protest at how they are discriminated against by the state.'

The level of poverty among the Bidun means that often there is no bread on the table. 'Women can't afford sanitary napkins. They can't afford nappies for their babies. Kuwaitis drive past these people in their Mercs, ignoring them living in the mud at the side of the road.'

Worse than anything, Hadeel says, is that 'the Bidun have no time for dreaming. Their aim is simply to get to the end of the day, alive.' As a direct response to this, Hadeel set up a workshop for the Bidun, to explore with them the importance of the imagination. She calls it 'Discover and Dream'.

It affords the Bidun recognition of their humanity, she believes. It offers them a safe place, some peace and the time to connect with others so that they can, for a while, escape the relentless daily struggle for survival.

Hadeel is adamant that another one of her government's displacement activities is to stir up fear and resentment. 'In that way, they succeed in dominating the population by stoking up fear of the "other". But the Bidun are not "other". We are all human beings. International solidarity is essential if we are to improve the lot of the Bidun.'

*

According to a recent Human Rights Watch report:

> Kuwait joined the Saudi-led coalition that began attacking Houthi and allied forces in Yemen on March 26, 2015, with media reporting that Kuwait had deployed 15 aircraft. Human Rights Watch has documented 87 apparently unlawful coalition attacks in Yemen, some of which may amount to war crimes, that killed nearly 1000 civilians and repeatedly hit markets, schools, and hospitals. Kuwait did not respond to Human Rights Watch inquiries regarding what role, if any, it has played in unlawful attacks in Yemen and if it was undertaking investigations into the role its own forces played in any of these attacks.[vii]

Kuwait, along with Saudi Arabia, the United Arab Emirates, Bahrain, Egypt, Morocco, Jordan, Sudan and Senegal is part of the coalition involved in the complex struggle in Yemen, a catastrophe that has been playing out since 2015. More than three million Yemenis have been displaced and two hundred and eighty thousand have sought asylum outside their own country. According to Al Jazeera reports, the USA, along with other Western powers such as the UK and France, has also supplied the Saudi-led coalition with weapons and intelligence.

*

Kuwait is a constitutional monarchy, with a single legislative body. Political parties are illegal. The ruling emir comes from the Ṣabāḥ family – which has ruled Kuwait since 1756 – and he rules the country through a council of ministers. The ministers come almost exclusively from the emir's own family and he himself appoints them to office. The National Assembly (Majlis al-Ummah) is responsible for legislation, and its fifty members are elected to four-year terms. This parliament was, however, suspended unilaterally by the Emir in 1976, in 1985, and again in 1999, in response to various internal political crises.

Recent analyses of events in Kuwait have noted a conservative Islamist backlash in response to any increase in 'westernisation'. There have been attempts to impose stricter religious codes and to limit foreign social influences. More women are covering themselves with the hijab, for example, or traditional veil, while hardliners try to ban social events like public concerts.

*

Continuing provisions in Kuwait's constitution, the national security law, and other legislation restrict free speech, and were used once again in 2017 to prosecute dissidents and stifle political dissent.

In January 2017, Kuwait carried out its first executions since 2013, hanging seven people.

Despite the repressive regime, Hadeel says, 'People are pushing for change. But international solidarity is essential. We can see the many dangers of a close US–Saudi friendship. And people are terrified of Iran; a fear that is routinely exploited by the government. Divide and conquer.'

*

Since we met in 2018, Hadeel has once again travelled to Lebanon and facilitated a training course on how to tweet safely. She continues to educate others at her own human rights training school in Kuwait. She continues to fundraise for stateless children in Kuwait. She continues to make herself available, on a daily basis, to the people who need her help. 'There are new cases, new causes, new files every day,' she says.

Her vision, above all, is to expand her school of human rights, to establish it as a prominent presence in her native Kuwait.

Spending those few days in Dublin in the autumn of 2018, feeling part of the large international community of human rights defenders everywhere, experiencing the support of Front Line Defenders has, Hadeel says, given her the impetus to carry on with her work, despite the dangers, despite the very real fear she experiences regularly, not just for herself, but also for her children.

'Pray for us,' she says.

There is so much work to be done.

[i] At the time of writing (November 2018), 1 KD equalled approximately €3.

[ii] Human Rights Watch, 'Kuwait: Events of 2018', *World Report 2019: Events of 2018*, Human Rights Watch, 2019, https://www.hrw.org/world-report/2019/country-chapters/kuwait#b94615

[iii] Ibid.

[iv] Mary Casey-Baker, 'Saudi Arabia issues warning against women's driving campaign', *Foreign Policy*, 25 October 2013, https://foreignpolicy.com/2013/10/25/saudi-arabia-issues-warning-against-womens-driving-campaign/

[v] Human Rights Watch, 'Kuwait: Events of 2018'.

[vi] Amnesty International, 'Kuwait 2017/18', *Amnesty International Report 2017/18: The State of the World's Human Rights*, London: Amnesty International, 2018, https://www.amnesty.org/en/countries/middle-east-and-north-africa/kuwait/report-kuwait/

[vii] Human Rights Watch, 'Kuwait: Events of 2017', https://www.hrw.org/world-report/2018/country-chapters/kuwait

LANA RAMADAN (Palestine)
written by Sheila O'Flanagan

The long dress is too big for me and the ends get grubby as we walk along the road. But it is our traditional dress and I am wearing it to connect with the people who have left. The people we had been. It is important to find that connection.

The other girls are wearing long dresses too. We look so tiny in them.

We are eleven years old.

When I see the cactus I pick some fruit. A long time ago houses were built beside cactus plants, but now the cactus is a sign of a destroyed village. This village has been destroyed like so many others. We have to walk through the dust and mud to find the ruined houses. Our dresses get even dirtier.

I take photographs, lots of photographs.

When we go back to the camp I show them to my grandfather. He looks at them all, and then he starts to cry. He can't stop.

'This is my house.' He points to one of the photographs. 'This is my house. I built it myself.'

I didn't know I had taken a photograph of his house, of his family's house, of a place where they lived, and ate. But the house is gone. Everything is gone. The people too. None of us can go back. Life in the village, the life of my parents and my grandparents, is over.

But I do go back, two more times, to see it. I have to make this journey to try to reconnect with the past and the shared memories. I don't have memories of the village but they are still a part of me in the same way that they are a part of my parents and my grandparents.

When, later still, I try to return once more, I can no longer find my grandfather's village. I stand on the top of the mountain and I look to where it should be, but I can't see the dusty road that we drove along before. It's completely hidden. The trees have taken over. That's why they plant them. So that we can't see. So that nobody can see. And so that nobody can go back.

My grandfather's memories were fragmented by Alzheimer's before he passed away. But his village, invisible from the road, was always there in his mind. People were forced from their villages. Nobody wanted to leave. He didn't want to leave. But they were not allowed to stay.

The Lost Villages

Neither my grandfather nor my grandmother was ready to go to the refugee camp when they left their home. They knew that to go there was to accept that they couldn't return. So they lived in a cave for a number of years. They didn't want to admit that they were refugees. But when their son turned six years old they wanted him to go to school. They wanted him to be educated. My grandfather was proud that he himself had received an education even though he had to go to the next village to be taught. But after he and my grandmother left their home, the only place their son could be educated was in the camp.

My parents knew all the soldiers who came there because they saw them every day. They knew their names and their nicknames. The nicknames were assigned to them before a raid and they used them to announce themselves when they arrived at the camp. Our parents resisted the soldiers – shouting at them, pushing them, and throwing stones. It was important to resist. It gave people something to be proud of. Yet many were killed or arrested. My parents were both arrested. It was part of their lives, part of my grandparents' lives and now part of our current life. One recent nickname that was used was 'Nidal'. 'Nidal' is an Arabic word and it means 'resistance'. It's a deliberately provocative nickname. They want to provoke us.

Over time the camp itself began to change. It was no longer a temporary place. It was becoming somewhere that people were growing up, being educated and learning about the world outside as well as the world inside. But just because they were in a different place, nobody forgot where they came from or how they ended up there, and nobody will forget. It is an inherited memory for my generation. Grandfather, father, son. Grandmother, mother, daughter. My father was detained before I was born but he never speaks about it. Our parents and grandparents don't want to talk about their lives before, but we carry their memories in our minds. And we hold tight to the same goals. We want freedom and our inherited rights.

We are educated people thanks to the strength of those who went before us. When I was a teenager I only wanted to dance but my parents wanted me to learn. And so I invested time in my education although I would have preferred to dance. When I was studying, I missed running around backstage and changing clothes and laughing with the other dancers. Dancing was a part of me. But it was very important to my mother and father that I had my education. They hated that I had to go away to study but they were so proud and so happy when I graduated. I did it for them.

*

When I go back, I am driven along a road. It's a modern road, big and wide. It's ten minutes from my house but until somebody else drove me along it, I didn't know it existed. It was built by the Israelis and it's in the West Bank, but it's not a road for Palestinians. If you look on Google Maps, you can see the names of many Palestinian villages surrounding the road. I know these villages. They exist. But when you drive on that road you don't see them. You don't see Palestinian people. There is nothing but the road. We are invisible and yet we are here.

It is not always easy. Sometimes you can despair. There was a time when I had no hope, and then a friend told me that even if we cannot make a change, we can build the basis for change. And he was right. You have to have faith. It doesn't have to be in God or in Palestine. It just has to be a belief. Something to keep you going. Because people have made sacrifices for you and for others. Some of those people have sacrificed their lives. And you are aware of that.

People deal with the situation in different ways. Sometimes they grow things in the garden. In the midst of all the destruction, to grow something is life-affirming. It is important to soothe the spirit in order to carry on. It is important to do something normal, something that you would do anywhere.

Being away is hard. Losing people when you're away is even harder. We are a social people, a social country. We share everything. When we're apart, when we cannot participate in family events, it hurts.

I get scared for my brothers and sisters who are still at home because they are teenagers and being a teenager in Palestine is difficult. But I think they're fine. I hope so. They're strong. They dance too, although I taught only one of them. I'm very proud of them.

I am a refugee. I am a dancer. I am educated. I work with human rights organisations and it is hard to deal with the arrests and the injuries when they are part of everyday life. When it is something that happens every day, every week, every month. But it is the right thing for me. We are grateful for international solidarity and the people who support us. It is always the people, not the governments. I can't see governments supporting us any time soon but people are pushing, again and again. And people make a difference.

This is my life. It is not my life alone. It's the life and the lives of the Palestinians I know. And we keep the shared memory for all of us.

The Past Seeps Up From Under

NURCAN BAYSAL (Turkey)
written by Lia Mills

This narrative has been compiled based on an extensive face-to-face interview held in Dublin in May 2018 and on information and quotes taken from Nurcan Baysal's blog and online journalism. It also draws information from official websites of various philanthropic, news and civil society organisations.

Around midnight one Sunday near the end of January 2018, a sudden explosion of noise shook the front door and the walls of Nurcan Baysal's home in Diyarbakır, a city in south-eastern Turkey. She thought it was an earthquake. Her second thought was that the house was being bombed. Then, as the walls crumbled, she realised it was the police, trying to batter their way through her front door. She shouted at her husband and a friend who happened to be there at the time – 'Take the children! Hide the children!' – as twenty masked men with Kalashnikovs burst in to her house.

'They carried the tools of war, as though making an assault on a major terrorist hideout. I thought they had come to kill me.' These armed and masked policemen told her they had a warrant to search her house. She asked if they had a warrant to knock down her door. They were surprised – people don't usually question them – but they said yes, they had a warrant. She asked to see it. No warrant was shown. Instead, they took her away to prison.

*

Nurcan (pronounced Nuur-jan, her name means 'full of light') was arrested because she posted a series of tweets condemning the Turkish government's military action in Afrin, a Kurdish enclave in north-west Syria, and calling for peace. She is a Kurd. She works on poverty, development and human rights issues, primarily as they affect the Kurdish population in Turkey, and her overall position is anti-violence, *tout court*. She is accused of promoting terrorist propaganda and calling for provocative action in her tweets.

Since her arrest, she has posted the five tweets that got her into trouble on her blog, to demonstrate that, far from calling for retaliation, they call for a cessation of violence. In one, she retweeted a photograph of a child who had been killed by a bomb with a message: 'Those who want war, look at this picture. This child died.'

In another tweet she called the government out on the code name they gave their military campaign: Operation Olive Branch. 'What are coming from tanks are not olive branches, they are bombs. When they drop, people are dying. Ahmet is dying, Hasan is dying, Rodi is dying, Mızgin is dying … Lives are ending …'

Her blog post continues, 'As you can see, these tweets do not contain any terrorist propaganda and I did not [call for], nor am I calling for, provocative action or violence. These tweets demonstrate that I am against war and death, and yes, I criticised the policies of the Turkish government.'

*

The special operations team brought her to their anti-terrorism department and put her in a cell, setting off an immediate wave of local and international protest from, for example, Human Rights Watch, writers' associations in Europe and women journalists' associations. The European Parliament issued a statement that included a reference to her case.[i] Hundreds of people in Diyarbakır – ordinary people who had benefited from her work and her support over years of activism – turned out and sat in the streets to protest her arrest, because of where she was held. There were mass protests on social media. These were not only members of the Kurdish party but people from across the political spectrum, even some right-wing people, she says. They were afraid for her, afraid of what might happen to her there. Almost six hundred people were detained in the same month but she was released after three days, pending a future trial. She believes the authorities let her go because so many people protested her arrest. That, combined with the level of international concern, made her case more visible than most.

*

Background

Nurcan's trial is due to take place on the morning that we meet in the conference room of the Front Line Defenders office in Dublin. Shortly after our meeting, she is due to collect a Front Line Defenders Global Laureate award from Kate Gilmore, UN Deputy High Commissioner for Human Rights, at a ceremony held in City Hall. There are journalists waiting outside to speak to her. She has an important event ahead of her. She is calm but she speaks quickly. She has serious things to say and not enough time to say them all. The threat of a prison sentence still hangs over her, not that you'd know it from her smile. The prosecutor wants her sentenced to three years for her five anti-war tweets. Just one hour before our meeting, her lawyer in Turkey managed to arrange for her hearing to be postponed. There is something truly extraordinary about this woman, about her life and the power of her presence. She doesn't seem aware of it herself. She sits, perfectly self-contained, and tells horrific stories in a matter-of-fact way.

 Of course, she has told these stories before. She'll go on telling them until something starts to change in the troubled world she comes from. Until some political conscience is jolted into action.

*

Nurcan grew up in a poor district of Diyarbakır, one of the largest cities in south-eastern Turkey, on a bluff overlooking the Tigris River, in what was once known as Mesopotamia. Its recorded history reaches back to the thirteenth century BCE but there is archaeological evidence that humans have lived there long before that. Its populations have included Assyrians, Armenians, Persians, Greeks, Romans, and the people of the Ottoman

Empire. The city has a population of almost a million people and is regarded by Kurds as the cultural centre and unofficial capital of Turkish Kurdistan. There are long-standing tensions between Kurds and the Turkish government.[ii] For a long time, most aspects of Kurdish culture were banned: their language; their music; the words 'Kurd', 'Kurdish', 'Kurdistan'; even, if you can believe it, certain letters of the Kurdish alphabet.[iii]

The old city of Diyarbakır is surrounded by substantial walls built by the Romans, and was, along with the Hevsel Gardens, granted UNESCO World Heritage status in 2015. But 2015 also saw the beginning of new disturbances in the region. In the 1990s, during intense conflict between the Turkish government and the Kurdistan Workers' Party (PKK), the population of Diyarbakır was dramatically increased by the forced migration of thousands of Kurds following the destruction of villages in the mountains by the state. The old city became crowded as it absorbed this displaced population.

*

Nurcan is one of ten children – a typical Kurdish family, she says. Her father is a grocer, her mother a housewife. She grew up in Şehitlik, a district in Diyarbakır that sees a great deal of poverty and violence. Even as a child, she was pragmatic and focused. When people asked what she wanted to be when she grew up, she told them she wanted to be mayor of Diyarbakır. 'My dream was mainly to study and leave Şehitlik, to have a good education and to return to my city.'

She and her siblings went to good schools and worked hard enough to get into an excellent high school – the criterion for attending her high school was not money, but performance in exams – and from there to win scholarships to university. In her district, they were the only people to do so. She studied political science at Ankara University, one of the most prestigious universities in Turkey, and then earned an MA at Bilkent University, where she stayed on to teach for a while. After five years in Ankara, Nurcan went back to Diyarbakır, the only one of her siblings to return.

Education, she says, is a way out of the world she grew up in. Most educated Kurds don't go back. She tries to understand this but it does make her angry, sometimes, that Kurdish people with ability and education go to the West and seem to forget what's happening in the region.[iv] Parents want their children to leave because life is dangerous for them there. Her decision to leave a good job at one of the most popular universities in Turkey and go back to Diyarbakır was so unusual it featured on the news. Because of her return, her father didn't speak to her for a year – but she didn't feel she had a choice. 'It's like when you see an accident. You can't walk on; you stop and do something. It's a human response.'

At first she worked for the UN Development Programme, managing projects on poverty and development. Then she worked for the Hüsnü M. Özyeğin Foundation, described on its website as 'a private foundation dedicated to promoting the social and economic development of Turkey by supporting initiatives in the fields of education, girls' empowerment, health and culture'. During these years she set up several civil societies (NGOs) to work on poverty and development issues, on women's issues and on the forced migration of Kurdish villagers. The development association she established in 2000 worked for the rights of displaced populations, the right of return and rural development. Villages were being burned, destroyed. People fled to the cities. 'I thought I had to do something,' she says. At that time, 'it was difficult to even say, "forced migration". Because then the question is: who forced them? And if you say, "the state", you've committed a crime.'

At that time, the Kurdish women's movement was growing and women were setting up NGOs. Nurcan used her education, training and experience to train others. Still working at her professional job, she used her salary to support the NGOs because Kurds in Turkey are so isolated that it's hard for them to find outside sponsorship or support. In 2011 she was part of a group of activists and academics – Turks as well as Kurds – who founded the Diyarbakır Institute for Political and Social Research (DİSA), which researches and records different aspects of the Kurdish experience in Turkey. Their aim is to study the experience of Kurds in Turkey with a view to finding solutions to problems and developing forward-looking policies.

These are their principles, as expressed on their website:

> DİSA is based on the fundamental principles of democracy, human rights and anti-discrimination. It will seek to bring together individuals of different points of view under the umbrella of these values and to facilitate their dialogue.
>
> DİSA sees the ethnic, religious, linguistic and other diversities within society as a source of richness. Thus, in all its studies, it will seek, as a matter of priority, the construction of an egalitarian social structure which will enable the peaceful co-existence of all differences, the construction of democracy and the restitution of justice and rule of law.[v]

Six years ago Nurcan left her job and began to write. Now, in addition to being an activist, a board member of several NGOs and an advisor to others, including groups working for peace in Turkey, she is a journalist, a blogger and a writer with several books to her credit. Her articles focus on human rights violations and on calls for peace. Her first book, *O Gün* (That Day), tells the story of the destruction of Kurdish villages in the mountains of south-east Turkey and the struggle to return, a struggle in which half of her high school class have died.[vi] She has co-authored a reference book that offers a guide to Kurdish civil society, the NGOs and the peace movement in Turkey. Everything she does in her working life is about social justice and advocacy. Every day she breaks a silence. Every day she speaks truth to power, but power, even when it is sympathetic to her cause (such as the European Parliament), doesn't seem to be listening. The power she threatens (her state) is a real and continuing threat to her. They don't want to hear what she says. They don't want other people to hear what she says either.

*

The Yazidis

In August 2014, Nurcan was on a beach holiday with her husband and children when ISIS attacked the Yazidis.

They cancelled their holiday. Her family went home and she went to Iraq. A post on her blog describes her first encounter with the displaced Yazidis:

> The moment we enter Zaxo, I see the Yazidis on the side of the road, in tents, or in construction sites. The Yazidis have made every empty construction in Zaxo a shelter to live in.[vii]

They got here through a humanitarian corridor opened and kept open by the YPG, the Kurdish youth movement. ISIS is everywhere, the women tell her. They say that many women committed suicide to avoid being taken. There are children everywhere, some sitting in dirty water. There are aid distribution points too. She goes into a half-finished building that houses thirty-nine Yazidi families, over two hundred people:

> Everywhere is full of children. Children are barefoot. By using stones and planks, they try to make a separate place for sleeping. Babies lie on the cushions put over the wooden planks. At one part of the building, a meal is being cooked in large, rusty pots. The backside of the building is used as a toilet. Clotheslines are being tied to the building. There are blankets and laundry being hung on those clotheslines. Everyone is under dust; everywhere is full of debris. A few women are washing clothes by hand using a wash bowl. Some old, sick, and disabled persons are lying on mattresses surrounded by debris. They are either barefoot or wearing slippers.

She asks people what they need. The Kurdish Regional Government supplies food and healthcare; the people of Zaxo have given them space to live safely. But conditions are far from ideal and will be worse when winter comes. Some of the buildings they live in are schools. What will happen when the schools need to re-open? Most people tell her they can never go back; their Arab neighbours betrayed them, cooperated with ISIS. One man says, 'We were killed by our neighbours.'

She moves on, past the UN camp where thousands of people are living, under the flags of UNHCR and UNICEF. Many Yazidis are also outside the camps and in ruined or unfinished buildings. In a similar site in Duhok, a more prosperous town hosting fewer Yazidis, there are women who stare at the wall with empty eyes. Children watch the life of luckier people out on the road: this building borders on an upmarket part of town, with smart cars, cafés, restaurants, a shopping and entertainment centre under construction. Nurcan sits down to talk with people who insist on giving her a cushion, 'probably the only one they have'. She asks if they resent the lives being lived out there across the road, in the cars and in the shops and cafés. They say no; the people of this town have taken them in, they are helpful. Their government brings food for the Yazidis to cook. They say they are the guests of the people who live there. 'Whatever they do for us, we say, God bless you.'

'There is a deep pain on everyone's face,' Nurcan writes. 'Even the babies and the children do not smile. I try to play jackstones with them, I try other games, but I cannot manage to make them laugh.' The children are living in an unfinished building on a luxurious street. They are 'hungry and thirsty, barefoot, sitting on the floor, and in between rubble. I cannot turn my back on them and go away.' But she must. One of the children cries when she leaves. Nurcan cries too.

This homelessness is so familiar to me. I cannot help crying loudly. Looking at those luxury cafés and restaurants, I cry for the whole world, the whole of humanity. I cry for the fate of Kurds. I cry for us being exiled from our lands throughout history, for our houses being collapsed on our heads, for our villages being burned, for our ever repeating homelessness. *How many, how many times?* I say to myself. *How many times have our houses been pulled down on our heads, and how many times have we had to build them up once again? … How many homes can you build in one lifetime?*

She is thinking about her much-loved uncle, Felat Cemiloğlu, who used to tell her stories of his experience of being uprooted and driven out of one home, starting again, only to be uprooted and driven out again. She explains:

In 1936, because of the Settlement Law, the Cemiloğlu family were forced to move to other provinces and other countries like Syria and Iraq. Felat Cemiloğlu, who was once the president of the Diyarbakır Chamber of Trade and Industry, pulled his teeth out by his bare hands as he was forced to eat his own stool in Diyarbakır Prison during the 12 September [1980] coup d'état period.

She began to organise aid for the Yazidis. For the next year and a half she volunteered in Yazidi camps. During that time she compiled testimonies of Yazidi women about what had happened to them and wrote about them in the newspapers so that people in Turkey would know what was happening, because some women told her they had been sold inside Turkey.

'There are always bad people but there are also always good people,' she says. Some Arabs and Kurds collected money to buy the women from ISIS and take them back to their families. But then there was a new problem, because the families did not always want to take those women back. There is a rule in Yazidi society that if a person has sex with someone who is not a Yazidi, even if she has been raped, she is no longer a Yazidi. Hundreds, maybe thousands, of Yazidi women have killed themselves. Nurcan wrote a book about this, entitled *Ezidiler: 73. Ferman* (Yazidis: 73rd Decree), which has since been banned in Turkish prisons.[viii] That's right. Only in the prisons. So far. There is no logic here. In response to the accusation that her book undermined the indivisible unity of the state of Turkey, she wrote a public statement asking why a book about the crimes of ISIS would be a threat to the indivisible unity of Turkey.

*

Diyarbakır

In 2015, after a period of peaceful negotiation and optimism during which some concessions were made (such as opening Kurdish departments in some universities and allowing Kurdish to be taught in some – but not all – schools and an election in which more than eighty Kurdish parliamentarians won seats), the war between the PKK and the Turkish state resumed. Rights were revoked.

When the clashes resumed, they didn't happen in remote areas in the mountains but in the cities. They happened in the heart of Diyarbakır, a city several thousands of years old, a World Heritage site, and home to almost a million people. Nurcan Baysal's city.

Young people from the Kurdish youth movement came down from the mountains, a traditional Kurdish stronghold, and joined young local Kurds to put up barriers and dig shallow 'trenches' in the streets, aimed at keeping state forces out of the old city. The police watched and did nothing. This went on for a while. Then, suddenly, a curfew was declared in Surici (Sur). A full-on, twenty-four-hour, seven-days-a-week curfew: an impossible restriction. Over time the curfew was extended to six different areas of the old city, known as Forbidden Zones. Anyone who went outside, for any reason or at any time, was in danger of being shot by special operations forces. Water and electricity were in short supply. For a while, access to the Internet was blocked. There was a comprehensive bombardment of streets where people were still living. The 'trenches' were cited as justification. But, people ask, why did the state not intervene sooner to put an end to those trenches? Why resort to such extreme violence as the bombing of people's homes?

The bombing and shooting happened in other cities too, cities with predominantly Kurdish populations, notably in Cizre, a town on the border between Turkey and Syria, as well as the six Forbidden Zones within the ancient city of Diyarbakır. People were killed in their homes by shrapnel or debris. Shrapnel decapitated one woman in front of her children while she was giving them breakfast.

The core of Diyarbakır is walled, with immense gates through which you enter the popular shopping area, the historic heart of the city. Throughout the curfew – the bombing, the shooting – protesters (politicians, intellectuals, journalists and human rights defenders) were at the gates. They tried to get inside the forbidden area but were blocked and hemmed in by special operations forces. The protests at the gates made no difference to what happened inside the city walls. During the protests, people were hurt, sometimes killed. Live, as well as rubber, bullets were used to subdue the protesters, along with tear gas and water cannons.

'Every day there were protests for Sur,' Nurcan says, '… mainly in Dağkapı Circle, at the entrance to Sur. Teachers, doctors, politicians, imams, students, workers, business people … people from different segments of the society. I was also participating in the protests. We had slogans like "walk to Sur", "stop the bombardment in Sur", "stop the curfew in Sur", "Sur, we are here", "Sur, you are not alone" … People were shouting slogans and clapping their hands while trying to walk to Sur. After ten to twenty minutes armed vehicles came and they began to use tear gas against the protestors. And we were trying to protect ourselves from tear gas. If the protestors still continued, after a while special operations teams would come. They were using black Ford Ranger cars. When Ford Rangers came we rushed into buildings, because special operations teams opened fire against protestors from those black Ford Rangers.'

Over a two-month period many people (mostly young protestors) were killed during the protests by shots from those Ford Rangers. 'We knew that protests would not stop the bombardment and death, but we wanted the people of Sur to hear our voices, not to feel alone, to know that at the other side of the city walls we were thinking of them.'

Those Voices
Those Voices, Nurcan Baysal's fourth book, tells the story of this extended curfew and the destruction of the eastern half of the old city from the point of view of different people who lived through it, witnessed it and survived it, including some who lived outside the Forbidden Zones. Some of the voices are Kurdish; some are Turkish. She gives a voice to the bombs as well. 'Boom! Boom!' is a refrain that punctuates the narrative, in which Nurcan starts each day in her office by adding to her count of the number of days the curfew has continued. We hear from people who live and work on either side of the city walls: men and women, Kurds and Turks, a teacher, a nurse, a car-park attendant, a student, housewives, mothers, fathers, children, siblings, neighbours – and merchants, including a jeweller. At one point it was estimated that 500 kg of gold was inside the forbidden area. A seventeen-hour ceasefire allowed business people to go in and rescue their goods while some residents packed what they could and left. Others refused to leave their homes, not believing the bombardment could continue. Other people wanted to leave but couldn't; they didn't have the money, or they had nowhere else to go and no way of getting there if they had.

One of the voices we hear is that of a man who went on hunger strike to try to force the authorities to order a ceasefire long enough for him to go out and retrieve the body of his brother, lying on open ground near the corpse of another young man. Nurcan first heard this story when she was organising a programme for an initiative called 'Defenders of the Peace' in December 2015. She and her colleagues went to the Governor to ask for help in retrieving the bodies. The families of the two young men went on hunger strike. Nurcan and her colleagues met them almost every day and went from institution to institution looking for information or help. They met the Prime Minister and Minister of Interior Affairs in Ankara. At last the prosecutor's office said that the bodies were in the morgue.

When eventually the families were allowed to reclaim them, the corpses were mutilated in such a savage way that Nurcan wishes she had never seen them: eyes and genitals gone; bodies ripped apart, disembowelled. It seemed that the corpses had been repeatedly shot – and possibly burned – post-mortem. Inevitably, animals had gotten to them. Some bodies were so degraded by the time they were recovered that they had to be stitched back together for burial. This prolonged exposure to indignity and the withholding of the right to decent burial causes unbearable torment to the families of the dead. One family is said to have kept the corpse of a child in their fridge for days.

The voices express dread, shame, despair, describing the death of human feeling that is the result of knowing what was happening and being unable to do anything about it. During the bombardment, European officials visited Turkey and left again. Nothing changed or stopped what was happening. It went on for months. You may have seen footage of some of it on your screens. You have certainly seen something similar. We are being inured to scenes of such appalling violence by overexposure. That's what Nurcan and people like her are up against – not only state violence and suppression but also a kind of global paralysis in the face of violence on such a scale.

What was Nurcan doing while her city was under bombardment? Besides continuing her work in journalism, besides raising a young family, besides protesting at the city gates, she was out there recording events, compiling testimonies; she was organising meetings at local government and government level, trying to facilitate a dialogue that would lead to peace. Here is a description in her own words, written in the context of her detention and release:

> I grew up with war in the city of Diyarbakır. I really do not know what a normal life looks like. I have spent my last twenty years struggling for peace, democracy, justice and freedom. I have established institutions, civil society organisations for a peaceful solution to the Kurdish issue. Even in the darkest days of 2015, during the bombardment in the heart of the Sur district of Diyarbakır, I was working towards opening a dialogue between the government and the Kurdish movement.

> I organised a number of meetings in my office, bringing members of the ruling party, the Kurdish movement and intellectuals together, trying to stop the deaths in the region. As a peace and human rights activist, my life has been spent dealing with forced migration, village guards, victims of mine accidents, poverty, women abducted by Islamic State, disarmament, dealing with dead bodies left in the streets, reporting war crimes and crimes against humanity.

> After three days [in prison] in the anti-terror department, I was released on bail, but I also received a travel ban. In the last week, an additional 311 people have been detained just for saying 'no' to war in Afrin. The state is trying to silence the voices against the war. They want all sectors of society, including the media, to support their war.

> As writers, activists, intellectuals and journalists, our responsibility is not to the state. We are responsible to our people, to humanity, to history, to life, to the Turkish and Kurdish youth who are dying now, to their mothers.[ix]

Voices in the Wilderness?

Nurcan Baysal and her colleagues, other human rights activists, run terrible personal risks to tell these stories, but to what effect? In another article, dated February 2018, Nurcan writes about moderating a panel at a conference held in the European Parliament two years earlier, during the bombardment of several cities in south-east Turkey. Her audience at the conference included parliamentarians. During her panel, she used her mobile phone to call a young man in Cizre, which was under heavy bombardment at the time. She connected her phone to the microphone so that everyone in the room could hear as this young man described being trapped – with others – in the basement of a building that had been destroyed by mortar fire. They had no water, no access to medical care. Several wounded people had already died; their bodies were still there. If the survivors tried to leave, snipers shot at them. He asked for help, for intervention with state forces. He reminded the European parliamentarians that they had enough power and influence to cause the siege of the town to be lifted. Nothing happened.

Nurcan doesn't describe the offices of the European Parliament where this conference took place. She doesn't have to. Picture the scene: a comfortable, airy space inside a vast building fronted by all the flags of member states. There is a lot of glass. There are security checks. A vast open lobby (very twenty-first century), climate-controlled meeting rooms, every modern means of communication available at the flick of a switch or click on a keypad. Plenty of coffee. Tasteful bite-size offerings for the breaks. The contrast could not be more stark. A young man speaking to this modern palace of democracy, communication and debate from a rubble-filled basement, under attack from lethal munitions deployed by a powerful state, pleading for his life and the lives of the other people crammed in there with him, among the dead bodies.

Ten days later, that young man and the people who were with him were burned alive. Casualty figures are disputed between the government and the NGOs but everyone agrees that, as well as combatants on both sides, many civilians were killed. At the same time, Nurcan's own city was under bombardment. She and her colleagues in human rights associations and other activists begged the European Parliament and European countries to do something to stop the shelling and the unreasonable, unliveable 24/7 curfew.

They tried to negotiate for humanitarian corridors that would allow people to leave safely, in groups, with civilian observers to inspect the process – just as they tried to negotiate a ceasefire so that bodies could be retrieved and buried. A time for such a corridor was agreed but when that time came, a fresh bombardment began instead. It is worth noting that when merchants needed to go in to Sur to retrieve goods and valuables from their shops, the ceasefire was honoured. At that time, some civilians did manage to leave, but others did not.

By the time military operations eased in the Forbidden Zones, by the time the bombardment stopped, the historical centre of Diyarbakır – a World Heritage Site, thousands of years old – had been destroyed. Other cities in the region suffered the same fate. Reduced to rubble, they were unrecognisable.[x] Elected mayors were accused of promoting or supporting terrorism; they were fired and replaced by state administrators. Some were imprisoned. After a failed military coup in July 2016, a state of emergency was declared. One hundred and fifty thousand people were fired from their jobs. Civil societies were shut down. Thousands of people were imprisoned. Along with censorship, travel restrictions came into effect. In her article describing all of this, Nurcan notes that Europe, still watching, is doing nothing. We're not waiting for you any longer, she writes. Now we know we are on our own.

*

In Plain Sight

In earlier conflicts in this region and other conflicts around the world (including Ireland) people have been 'disappeared' by one side or another. There is a difference between such acts, which are by their nature hidden, and what happened in Diyarbakır and Cizre – or, indeed, in the case of the ISIS attack on the Yazidis – where the killing and destruction happened in full view. The whole world could watch if it chose, via the news and social media.

There is an expression that recurs in accounts of the destruction of Diyarbakır: *But, the trenches …* It is used to qualify or justify the severity of the state measures taken in the centre of the city. It is a kind of spin, asserting that terrorists were hiding and operating in the old city; they were the state's legitimate targets, they are to blame, they put the civilian population at risk. Some Kurds share this view. But the destruction was wholesale and extreme. It was clear that the shelling was indiscriminate, that ordinary people were being killed.

The effect on the inhabitants of the rest of Diyarbakır, outside the old city walls, was paralysing. They describe feelings of helplessness and shame. One woman explains that even as you try to keep things normal for your children, all the joy has gone from life. How can you celebrate a child's birthday when you know children are starving and dying on the other side of the wall, where there is little water (the tanks had been damaged) and no electricity? From the windows and terraces of safer houses that used to have enviable views over the old town, people could see fires and smoke rising as Sur collapsed. They knew there were dead bodies left out in the open on streets they used to walk. And the noise: under bombardment, women miscarry. One woman describes trying to get out of her house to find milk for her hungry baby and being turned back by soldiers.

Even children who live in safer parts of town are badly affected. Fearful and jumpy, they are afraid that they will die with each explosion. Their eardrums burst. Time is distorted. One woman describes missing important exams because she lost track of days. Another describes going to the mortuary to collect the body of her eighty-three-year-old mother, who has died of natural causes, and feeling shame when she sees a family who are there at the same time to mourn the broken body of a young man. She doesn't think she has a right to grieve her elderly mother in those circumstances.

How did the activists and protesters feel in those days? They were doing everything they could to stop the bombardment, to find a way to talk about peace, but getting nowhere. Nurcan says, 'After a while, you feel worthless. You understand that your life and the lives of people in Sur are unworthy in the eyes of the state. We knew that we were killable, and this feeling accompanies you all the time. Beside all these cruelties, life continued under the sounds of bombs, fireworks, guns and armoured vehicles. And you feel deeply ashamed of yourself, because while people are dying, your life continues. You become angry with yourself and with everyone.' These emotions were common, she says. 'Helplessness and shame always accompany you: shame of living.

'People who don't have a war experience have no idea what it's like to live in war. … When a bomb drops, life stops for a minute, but then it continues … Children go to school, parents go to work, ill people are taken to hospitals, we drink coffee and sometimes we even make jokes under the bombardment, through tear gas and protests. War becomes part of your life.

'During those bombardment days, I took an active role in informing the public about the human rights violations and the war crimes with my articles. Mainstream Turkish media have closed their eyes to the ongoing war and human rights violations happening in our cities. I also took an active role in stopping these crimes. I organised several meetings with NGO leaders and members of the Kurdish movement and discussed how we can save the lives of the people trapped in the bombardment area. I documented the human rights abuses and stayed in the bombardment area with the families to increase public awareness of the bombardment and the deaths. I also worked to retrieve the dead bodies that were on the ground and being eaten by animals. A few times, with other activists, we tried to enter the curfew area to retrieve the dead bodies, but the special operation teams shot at us. I also organised solidarity campaigns for the people who lost their houses and family members.

'Amidst all my struggle, I had the same feeling: shame. Shame of living, shame because my life continued, shame that I could eat, drink, while people were dying. Today, people still have those feelings. Six districts of Sur were totally destroyed, we not only lost our children but also half our city, a city that is seven thousand years old, a city that was the heart of Mesopotamia. People think they should have done more to stop the war. But we couldn't.'

*

Personal Cost?

In her article about the absence of European intervention, Nurcan Baysal writes, 'We have given up waiting [for outside help]. We are on our own.' But in reality, the world's awareness does matter. If not for the reaction of the people she has worked amongst and for throughout her adult life, if not for the protests of international NGOs and the express concern of the European Parliament, Nurcan could be still in jail awaiting trial – as so many of her compatriots are, as so many journalists around the world are. One night she got a call from a friend who was expecting to be arrested. 'I told her to prepare a small bag with a towel, slippers, toothbrush, medicine and clothes to keep warm.'

Imagine preparing a prison bag and packing essentials, for all the world like a bag a person would pack if she were about to have a baby.

'Today, there are no bombs dropping in the city centres. But there is heavy state pressure, thousands of people are in prison, arrests continue and people live in fear. There is a big silence. Inside this silence, we continue to struggle.

'A while ago, on a music channel on TV, between music videos, the host said that the police should shoot the people who are against the war in Afrin whether they are parliamentarians, businessmen, or journalists.

'In another popular entertainment programme, hosts have targeted one hundred and seventy intellectuals who signed a letter against the war in Afrin. In the programme, they read the letter sentence by sentence with the pictures of the signatories. The hosts labelled these intellectuals as "traitors" and said that those traitors do not have a right to live in this country; they should be expelled from the country. One of the signatories' job contract was ended by her university because of the letter.

'A campaign on www.change.org has been launched against these one hundred and seventy "traitors" to revoke these "terror-lovers'" Turkish citizenship. I am also one of those "traitors" that signed the letter and I really don't know where to go. This is my country, my land, my home and I don't want to leave. And yes, I am against war!'

She says that it's only a matter of time until they come for her. She can't allow herself to think about it. Every day she wakes up and checks to see who has been detained overnight, who has left the country. Nearly all of her friends have left, they are in Europe now. Many people and organisations want her to leave, she has been invited to live in Europe with her children, but she doesn't want to go; that's what the state wants her to do.

What do her children think about what she does? They know everything, she says. You can't lie to children. And it's all out there on social media anyway, abuse and threats and accusations: *terrorist bitch, we will rape you* … She has explained to them that if she goes to prison, it won't be for committing a crime but because of her work for peace and for human rights, for their own people. And they hear from other people who are proud of her. The children are proud of her too but sometimes angry, because she could stop at any time, if she chose. She says many people work the way she does; she's not the only one. She had a choice once: she could have stayed away but she came back. She has a choice now: she could leave. She doesn't.

'But it's a struggle, you know. It's a struggle. Sometimes people are so hopeless, in my region especially, because now they live in too much silence. It is hard for people to say anything; they turn into themselves, people don't even go outside because they are in shock. I am shouting and talking and talking. I tell them: it's like a river, freedom. Sometimes it flows in silence but it flows.'

Is she afraid? She doesn't want to think about it. She's not afraid for herself but for the children, for the future, for future generations. 'I don't want them to have the same life. It should stop somewhere, you know? A hundred years is too much. So, you know, it's not because I am courageous, it's because I am stupid. I don't think about it. Sometimes I ask myself: Nurcan, why are you like this?' She laughs. 'I will not think about it, I will not do that to myself. When you are afraid, others are afraid. It's like an illness, you know? It spreads to everyone. But when you show courage, that also spreads to other people. It gives power to other people.'

The work that has endangered her could also save her. Because her international profile is so high, because of the many prizes she has won for peace work and for her work in development and with women's groups, the state knows that people outside their borders are watching. This is why the wider work of human rights organisations, like Amnesty International, PEN International and Front Line Defenders, matters. If, reading this, you feel powerless – you have some power, at least. You can support those organisations and get involved.

This is what democracy is for, using your voice to protest against injustice and celebrate the people who fight it and keep us informed.

One of the weapons of officialdom is the not-so-subtle use of language that controls our perception and evades responsibility for its actions. 'Terrorists' (sometimes 'vermin'; sometimes 'infidels') are 'neutralised' or 'contained', while 'heroic' soldiers 'sacrifice' their lives. There is a cruel irony at work when a military operation is called 'Olive Branch'. Listening to these stories, we must always be alert to bias, watch where value is assigned and where it is not and correct for balance. A life is a life.

If not for the few brave people like Nurcan Baysal, who continue to bear witness to the reality of what happens, it would be easy for us to accept the official line, that terrorists are holding the local population to ransom and that governments, armies, have no choice but to take punitive action. She reminds us that there is always a choice. She names things for what they are. *This is war. This is a dead child. That was my hometown. These people were burned alive.*

Nurcan writes that peace must come, eventually. It has to. The sooner all concerned put aside their weapons and sit down to talk about how that can be brought about, the better.

*

There is a spectacularly chilling passage in Nurcan's book, *Those Voices*, where a teacher describes trying to teach her class the finer points of grammar during a bombardment. Subject, predicate, object: direct and indirect. In the text, the teacher speaks, and then the bombs speak.

Now, children, she asks. What is the hidden object of this sentence?

Boom! Boom!

Nurcan Baysal is the 2018 Front Line Defenders winner of the Global Laureate Award for Human Rights Defenders at Risk. On 21 February 2019, the 7th Criminal Court of First Instance of Diyarbakır acquitted Nurcan Baysal of 'inciting the public to hatred and enmity' charge. The acquittal decision is final.

i '[T]he crackdown on political dissent through social media continues; whereas 573 people, including activist Nurcan Baysal and members of the Executive Committee of the Turkish Medical Association, were detained for posting comments on social media that were critical of the Turkish government's military incursion in the Syrian enclave of Afrin', 'European Parliament resolution on the current human rights situation in Turkey (2018/2527(RSP)', Item O, http://www.europarl.europa.eu/sides/getDoc.do?type=MOTION&reference=B8-2018-0091&language=EN; accessed 16/07/2018. 573 is the number released on 5 February. According to the Ministry of Internal Affairs' statement on 19 February 2018, since the launch of the military operations on 20 January, Turkish authorities have taken 786 people into custody on accusations of 'terrorist propaganda' for being part of protests and events or sharing social media posts opposing Turkish military intervention in Afrin. Members of the Turkish Medical Association were not detained over social media posts; they were detained in relation to their press release opposing the Turkish military intervention in Afrin.

ii There has been violent conflict between the Turkish state and the Kurdistan Workers' Party (PKK) since the late 1970s, except for a period of ceasefire (2013–15) during which a democratic solution seemed possible. Many Kurds want an independent Kurdistan but many simply want the right to speak their own language and freely enjoy their own culture within the state of Turkey.

iii During a cessation of hostilities prior to the 2015 election, these restrictions eased for a while but they seem to be on the way back.

iv Kurdistan as a region used to be a buffer between the Ottoman and Persian empires. After World War I, it was divided between four countries: Turkey, Iraq, Syria and Iran. Some Kurds throughout the region agitated for a separate independent country. In Turkey, throughout years of conflict, Kurdish culture and language have been suppressed. Kurds are estimated to constitute fifteen to twenty per cent of the overall population of Turkey.

v 'The Principles of the Institute', DİSA, http://www.disa.org.tr/about us&q=46&id=51&t=7&k=29&ln=en_EN&sq=2; accessed 30/07/2018.

vi *O Gün* is not yet available in English but reviews, extracts and discussions are available online.

vii Nurcan Baysal, 'Yazidis: 74th Firman', *Nurcan Baysal: Blogspot*, 5 December 2014, http://nurcanbaysal.blogspot.com/2014/12/yazidis-74th-firman.html

viii *Yazidis: 73. Ferman* (Yazidis: 73rd Decree). In this context, 'decree' means genocide. Nurcan explains that many communities have subjected Yazidis to decrees: 'There is a saying in Mesopotamia, if a person wants to mention all the communities/nations of the world, "72 nations/ communities of the world". For example, "72 communities/nations believe x", meaning "the whole world believes x". So, for Yazidi people, "subjected to decrees by 72 communities/ nations of the world" means that all the nations of the world committed atrocities against them, throughout history. So, the last decree, the last genocide by ISIS, is the 73rd decree for them. Every morning, when they wake up, Yazidis turn to the sun and they pray to God: "My God, protect the 72 communities of the world and also protect us."'

ix Nurcan Baysal, 'The price of saying "no" to war in Turkey', *Ahval News*, 1 February 2018, https://ahvalnews.com/peace/price-saying-no-war-turkey; reposted on https://www.opendemocracy.net, February 2018.

x A 'regeneration'/gentrification programme is already underway.

SEHAM OSMAN (Egypt)

written by **Melatu Uche Okorie**
artwork by **Rosa Devine**

CAIRO

NUBIA IS A REGION IN THE SOUTH OF EGYPT, THE INDIGENOUS HOME OF THE NUBIAN PEOPLE – AN ETHNOLINGUISTIC GROUP BELIEVED TO HAVE LIVED IN SOUTH EGYPT AND NORTHERN SUDAN FOR OVER 4000 YEARS.

BETWEEN 1900 AND 1970, AN ESTIMATED 50,000 NUBIANS WERE FORCED FROM THEIR ANCESTRAL HOMES ALONG THE NILE AS A RESULT OF DAM CONSTRUCTION PROJECTS.

ASWAN

ALTHOUGH MANY WERE MOVED TO 'TEMPORARY' ACCOMMODATION, THEIR DESCENDANTS ARE STILL CAMPAIGNING FOR PERMISSION TO RETURN TO THEIR ANCESTRAL LAND.

IN NOVEMBER 2016, NUBIAN RIGHTS DEFENDERS IN ASWAN ORGANISED A 'NUBIAN CARAVAN,' DRIVING DOZENS OF CARS TOWARDS THEIR INDIGENOUS NUBIAN LANDS, MUCH OF WHICH HAD BEEN PLACED UNDER MILITARY CONTROL.

SEHAM OSMAN, THE FIRST WOMAN TO RUN FOR THE PRESIDENCY OF THE NUBIAN UNION, WAS INVOLVED IN THIS PROTEST MOVEMENT.

FOR HER, THERE IS NO DISCONNECT BETWEEN WOMEN'S RIGHTS AND LAND RIGHTS. HER WORK INVOLVES A LOT OF ADVOCACY FOR AND WITH WOMEN AND GIRLS IN HER COMMUNITY.

40

I MET WITH SEHAM AT THE OFFICES OF FRONT LINE DEFENDERS IN DUBLIN. IT'S HER SECOND VISIT TO IRELAND, A COUNTRY THAT SHE DESCRIBES AS 'VERY NICE' AND A PLACE THAT SHE DOES NOT GET LOST IN BECAUSE 'THE PEOPLE ARE HELPFUL.'

I HAD ALREADY SEEN SEHAM SPEAK AT TRINITY COLLEGE THE PREVIOUS THURSDAY AND I WAS VERY EXCITED TO MEET HER.

...YOU WERE TALKING ABOUT WOMEN'S RIGHTS, AND THAT INTERESTED ME A LOT. I'M SO HAPPY, SO GRATEFUL THAT YOU COULD COME OUT FOR ME TODAY AND TALK TO ME.

WOMEN' RIGHTS IS AN INTEREST OF MINE, AND EVERYTHING YOU WERE SAYING, I WAS LIKE, YES, YES, YES...'

THANK YOU!

SO; WE WANT TO KNOW ABOUT YOU. COULD YOU TALK A LITTLE ABOUT YOURSELF AND YOUR UPBRINGING?

I AM FROM A NUBIAN FAMILY, BORN AND RAISED IN ASWAN, A CITY IN EGYPT WHICH BORDERS SUDAN. I COME FROM A SMALL FAMILY, BOTH PARENTS STILL LIVING.

I WENT THROUGH ALL THE LEVELS OF MY EDUCATION IN ASWAN AND OBTAINED A BACHELOR OF SCIENCE IN MATHEMATICS AND A TWO-YEAR TEACHING DIPLOMA. I TEACH MATHS TO PRIMARY STUDENTS.

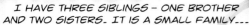

I HAVE THREE SIBLINGS – ONE BROTHER AND TWO SISTERS. IT IS A SMALL FAMILY...

BUT I ALSO HAVE AN EXTENDED FAMILY WITHIN MY NUBIAN TRIBE, ALL LIVING IN ASWAN.

SEHAM AND HER SISTER AYAT ARE FOUNDING MEMBERS OF GENOUBIA HORA.

HOW DID THAT START?

ALTHOUGH I HAD BEEN INVOLVED IN ACTIVISM FOR A LONG TIME BEFORE GENOUBIA HORA, THIS ORGANISATION HAD ITS ORIGINS IN THE JANUARY 2011 UPRISING IN EGYPT. THE REVOLUTION STARTED BECAUSE WE WANTED HOSNI MUBARAK, WHO HAD BEEN THE PRESIDENT OF EGYPT FOR THIRTY YEARS, TO LEAVE. THERE WAS EXTREME POVERTY, UNEMPLOYMENT AND LACK OF FREEDOM OF EXPRESSION IN EGYPT, AND PEOPLE WANTED THE REGIME AT THE TIME, SPECIFICALLY PRESIDENT MUBARAK, TO STEP DOWN.

BUT AFTER THE REVOLUTION, WE WOMEN WHO HAD PROTESTED ALONGSIDE THE MEN, GONE ON MARCHES AND EVEN HELPED TO DEVELOP AND COORDINATE STRATEGIES REGARDING THE REVOLUTION, FOUND THAT WE WERE NOT BEING TAKEN SERIOUSLY AND THAT OUR OPINIONS WERE NOT BEING TAKEN INTO CONSIDERATION.

IT WAS JUST THE MEN WHO WERE MAKING ALL THE DECISIONS.

SO, IN 2012, WE DECIDED TO FORM GENOUBIA HORA.

WHAT HAVE YOU BEEN WORKING ON?

ONE OF OUR SUCCESSFUL CAMPAIGNS HAS BEEN THE RELEASE OF OUR FELLOW NUBIAN ACTIVISTS, THIRTY MEN AND WOMEN WHO WERE IMPRISONED FOR PEACEFULLY PROTESTING FOR THE RIGHTS OF NUBIANS, THROUGH SOCIAL MEDIA CAMPAIGNS, REPORTS ISSUED BY AMNESTY INTERNATIONAL AND FRONT LINE DEFENDERS, THE ACTIVISTS WERE RELEASED. BUT THEY ARE STILL FACING CHARGES.

AND YOUR WORK FOR WOMEN'S RIGHTS? GENOUBIA HORA IS LED BY WOMEN, FOR WOMEN. WHAT WORK DO YOU DO IN THIS AREA, AND WHAT ARE THE ISSUES?

I HAVE HAD TO LEARN A LOT IN THIS AREA. INITIALLY, WHEN WE STARTED GENOUBIA HORA, I HAD THOUGHT THAT EVERY GIRL WAS LIKE ME, THAT THEY COULD TAKE PART IN SOLIDARITY ACTIONS AND MARCHES, BUT I QUICKLY REALISED THAT SOME GIRLS IN ASWAN WERE NOT EVEN ALLOWED TO GO TO SCHOOL. ONE OF OUR MAIN AREAS OF WORK BECAME TO RAISE AWARENESS AROUND WOMEN'S RIGHTS AND DOMESTIC VIOLENCE.

WE DEVELOPED A BOOKLET ON DOMESTIC VIOLENCE DOCUMENTING THE STORIES OF WOMEN AND GIRLS FROM ASWAN, AND DID WORKSHOPS IN THE FIVE DIFFERENT REGIONS IN ASWAN TO RAISE AWARENESS ABOUT FORMS OF HARASSMENT. WE ALSO DISPLAYED ARTWORK BY SOME OF THE WOMEN AND GIRLS ABOUT THEIR EXPERIENCES OF SEXUAL HARASSMENT.

THAT'S A LOT TO TAKE ON.

THE JOB DOES BECOME DIFFICULT FOR US.

SOME OF US NOTICED THAT WE WERE BECOMING DEPRESSED FROM LISTENING TO ALL THE STORIES OF ABUSE, SO WE SET UP A GOOD SUPPORT SYSTEM FOR OURSELVES. IT'S IMPORTANT TO REALISE THAT SOMETIMES WE HAVE TO SEEK SUPPORT FOR OUR OWN MENTAL WELL-BEING.

THEREFORE, WE TRY TO ORGANISE TRIPS WHERE WE GO OUT FOR THE WEEKEND. THERE ARE ALSO LEISURE TRIPS WITH THE GIRLS INSIDE ASWAN, WHICH THE GIRLS WOULD USUALLY REQUEST, AND SOMETIMES WE DO ZUMBA.

DELEGATING IS EQUALLY IMPORTANT. WE HAVE NETWORKS OF GROUPS MADE UP OF MOSTLY YOUNGER GIRLS WITHIN THE DIFFERENT MUNICIPALITIES INCLUDING CAIRO.

I TRY TO SPLIT MY DAY TO INCORPORATE MY WORK BOTH AS A TEACHER AND MY JOB WITH GENOUBIA HORA.

I TEACH FROM MORNING UNTIL 2PM; I REALLY ENJOY MY JOB AS A TEACHER. I THINK THAT THERE IS A LOT OF INTERPLAY BETWEEN MY WORK AS A TEACHER AND MY WORK IN ACTIVISM.

AND FROM 2PM TO 7PM, I WORK WITH GENOUBIA HORA.

SOMETIMES, I WORK BEYOND 7PM IF I HAVE EXTERNAL MEETINGS.

HOW DO YOU FIND TIME FOR EVERYTHING?!

THIS IS THE PROBLEM WITH MY LIFE!

IT IS ESPECIALLY DIFFICULT WHEN I HAVE TO TRAVEL ABROAD FOR LONG PERIODS OF TIME.

YES, WE STILL DRINK COFFEE!

THE LAST QUESTION I HAVE FOR YOU – IF SOMEONE FROM ANOTHER VILLAGE WANTS TO SET UP SOMETHING LIKE YOU HAVE, WHAT ADVICE WOULD YOU GIVE TO THEM?

AND WHAT IS NEXT FOR YOU?

WE TELL OUR YOUNGER GIRL GROUPS THAT EVEN IF THEY HAVE MALE MEMBERS, THEY SHOULD ALWAYS TRY TO MAINTAIN A FEMALE MAJORITY BECAUSE THEIR GROUPS ARE THE ONLY SPACES WHERE THE FOCUS IS ON THE DEVELOPMENT OF GIRLS. WE ENCOURAGE THEM TO HAVE WOMEN IN LEADERSHIP ROLES.

WE ADVISE THEM TO AVOID BURNOUTS AND TAKE BREAKS WHEN NEEDED – TO ALWAYS HAVE A LOT OF VOLUNTEERS AROUND IN CASE OF ANY DANGER, AND TO HAVE SOMEONE TO SPEAK TO IN CASES OF EMERGENCY.

I WILL CONTINUE TO CAMPAIGN FOR THE NUBIAN ACTIVISTS WHO WERE IN PRISON FOR PEACEFULLY PROTESTING FOR THE RIGHT OF RETURN FOR NUBIANS.

I WILL ALSO CONTINUE TO PROVIDE SUPPORT TO WOMEN IN DIFFICULT SITUATIONS. WE CAN PROVIDE THEM NOT ONLY WITH LEGAL AID, BUT ALSO WITH A SPACE AND A PLACE TO TALK ABOUT THINGS. WE FIND THAT EVEN EMOTIONAL SUPPORT AND MENTAL WELL-BEING ARE VERY IMPORTANT IN THESE CASES.

On 7 April 2019, Seham Osman, along with seven other defendants in the case known as the 'Dofof Trial' were acquitted by the Aswan Misdemeanour State Security Emergency Court. Twenty-five other Nubian human rights defenders who were prosecuted in the case, including Maysara Abdoun and Mohamed Azmy, were handed a suspended fine of 50,000 EGP (approx. €2,600) each. To come into effect, the court's decision needs to be ratified by the president.

MUNA HASSAN MOHAMED (Somalia)
written by **Azra Naseem**

'One of my best friends lost sight in both eyes in a car explosion two weeks ago,' Muna Hassan tells me on the phone from Mogadishu. 'I am sorry I couldn't take your call when you rang.'

It is April 2019. Violent death and devastating injuries routinely interrupt daily life in the Somalian capital. About a hundred people a month, roughly a thousand a year, are killed nationwide. Poets are murdered for their verses; writers for their words; politicians for their pledges; clerics for their prayers. Homosexuals and lesbians stoned; children put to death by the state; girls genitally mutilated; women raped, assaulted, made into spoils of war; youth weaponised, turned into explosives that maim and kill themselves and others. Warring factions, sections, tribes, states. Divided and armed. The brutal 'holy warriors' of al-Shabaab. Local soldiers. Foreign troops. Peacekeepers. Paramilitaries. Contractors. Drones. Trump.

'Caught in the crossfire' – shunted between the good, the bad and the stupid, the inept leaders who fail to protect, the sexual predators in soldiers' fatigues, the 'Jihadists' that commandeer conscience and kidnap faith, foreign leaders with more firepower than brainpower – the people of Mogadishu feel stifled, unable to breathe, too terrified to move. But move they must. Close to three million people, half of them women and children, are internally displaced; homeless, rootless, at serious risk of abuse, unassisted.

Somalia is one of the worst places to be human in the twenty-first century. Muna Hassan is a human rights defender in Somalia.

Twenty-nine-year-old Abukar Ahmed Mohamud Hassan was passing by when a car bomb went off. 'He is one of my best friends. He has three children. He can no longer see,' Muna laments on the phone. There is no time for pleasantries. Life is too short for small talk.

'We cannot go on like this. We are prisoners here, in this city,' Muna is angry. I can hear it in her voice. 'I have to do something.'

Muna and I began our conversation a year ago – a short conversation over a long time.

'Of course, I will talk to you, Sister,' she laughed warmly when I first sought her permission to probe.

My name, with its Arabic roots, earned me what I felt was an undeserved kinship. The warmth of Muna's welcome has not changed over the year. Whenever we talk, she is eager to discuss her work, proud of it, bristling with purpose.

Today's phone call, eleven months after we first talked, is intended to close open brackets, conclude fragmented sentences and tie loose ends.

Muna has other plans.

'I am going to meet the Prime Minister tonight. I am going to tell him, and the Minister of State for Security – he will be there too. I will tell them. This has to change. We need freedom.'

She sounds firm, determined.

The meeting is less than two hours away. A new chapter is opening in Muna's story. This is not the time for neat conclusions. Will there ever be such a time? Muna's life is too full of purpose and action, of danger and ambition. It cannot be neatly packaged for ease of comprehension.

I will call another time to dot my i's and cross my t's.

Muna arrived in Mogadishu five years ago, from the Beledweyne District in the Hiran region, some three hundred kilometres away. A woman in her thirties with alert black eyes, a beaming smile, and a terrorist group at her heels.

Today Muna is recognised as the most influential voluntary youth activist in Somalia and has won many accolades for her voluntary work as a youth leader.

When she was nine years old, her father was killed by clan militias who unjustly accused him of betrayal by siding with rivals. Somalia: from Cold War straight to civil war, followed by failure as a state, armed clan rivalries, famine, peacekeepers, foreign interventions, and now armed religious militants. Twenty years of relentless violence.

Muna remembers little else. Violence outside, violence inside.

'It was not the best life,' Muna is dispassionate with the personal.

'To buy us our daily bread', Muna recalls life without her father, 'my mother had to work all day.'

Muna spent the time in the care of her grandmother.

They took her to a village elder one day, the mother and the grandmother. They had her labia minora and majora cut with a sharp instrument before sealing shut her vaginal orifice.

The seal is formed, experts say, by cutting and repositioning the labia minora and/or the labia majora. This can take place with or without removal of the clitoris.

Infibulation, it is called.

'They were some of the most painful days of my life,' Muna recalls.

Infibulation can lead to complete vaginal obstruction, trapping inside the menstrual flow or, as in Muna's case, urine.

'They sewed me back too severely. For three days I was unable to pee.'

A doctor had to cut her open. Torn twice within a week. The flesh no longer feels the pain; the mind holds it close.

Somalia is one of twenty-five countries in Africa where people still practise female genital mutilation (FGM), the removal of the external female genitalia or other injury to the female genital organs for cultural or other non-medical reasons.

Shortly after Muna and I talk about how she was cut, FGM in Somalia becomes world news. A young girl of ten, Deeqa Dahir Nuur, bleeds to death after being cut in a remote village in July 2018.

'It should not be a part of our culture,' say politicians in response.

'It is our culture,' says Deeqa's father, unapologetic on Voice of America.

'It is not just today, or yesterday. It is every day,' says Muna.

Two months later, new headlines: Aasiyo and Khadijo Farah Abdi Warsame, aged ten and eleven, die after FGM in a remote pastoral village in Somalia's Puntland.

In every society that ritually mutilates women, say observers, the practice is a manifestation of deeply entrenched gender inequality.

What they know from watching, Muna knows from experience. That is why she spends much of her time facilitating possibilities for the empowerment of women.

Women in Somalia are downtrodden. 'Underdeveloped,' Muna says. Without question, few Somali women get to reach their full potential as human beings – there are few places in the world where women are worth as little in comparison to men as in Somalia.

The world's gender inequality index puts Somalia in fourth position. Gender-based violence against women is common in and out of the home. Violence suffered by women in their own homes goes mostly unreported; most of what is reported goes unpunished. Out in the fluid battlefields of al-Shabaab's asymmetrical warfare, women are raped, turned into sex-slaves, vessels for bearing children, as far from equal as can be.

'I meet with rape victims regularly. There are more every day. The perpetrators include government forces. I have raised this issue with politicians.' Muna feels the women's pain, and empathy softens her voice. Sisterhood. Respect for human dignity. Indignation at its absence.

'There is no justice. There is no justice.' Muna repeats. 'I have raised the matter with the Minister for Women.' Muna's lobbying is tireless.

'We are all in this together. We are developing. We will get there.' She receives platitudes in return.

Muna does not allow the ugly to be hidden. 'I have raised the issue of abuses by government forces,' she says.

Unlawful killings by security forces are common, report human rights monitors. They are also involved in rape and forced evictions, fraud, corruption.

'Mistakes have been made,' officials high up have admitted to Muna. 'Things need to change.'

Rhetoric that will remain nothing but? Muna chooses to be optimistic.

'There is sincerity,' she believes. 'They just don't understand local dynamics.'

'Most of the government is foreign,' Muna says with a hint of disapproval. 'Diaspora.'

She chooses not to dwell on the negative impact of such governance, discussing instead how it presents an opportunity for her, as a youth leader, to inform policy by sharing her local knowledge.

Muna will, therefore, continue proposing plans, suggesting strategies, imploring for improvement, pushing for progress. 'Somalians deserve better.'

While political prevarications draw people further into Somalia's quagmire of insecurity, while traditions are allowed to trample human rights, mutilated girls continue to form their wounds. Between 2015 and 2030, the UN estimates, 68 million girls will be cut in Africa. How can such a large-scale assault be prevented?

'Changing how people think, that is the key,' Muna says. The norm must become abnormal; ritual must become taboo.

Muna has an eight-year-old daughter, Istabraq, and a fifteen-year-old son, Omer. They live with her mother, back in the village where Muna lived as a child. Where she was cut.

'Do you have reservations about leaving your daughter with your mother?' I am hesitant about the question, but ask anyway. Loss of trust in caregivers is common among girls made to undergo FGM.

'My mother no longer believes what she believed then,' Muna tells me with confidence. 'We learn, we grow, we change. She knows now it was not the right thing to do.'

Muna has gone boldly where psychologists say most adults cannot – rebuilding trust in the caregivers who caused them harm as children.

Strong willpower. The ability to confront trauma and emerge from it stronger. The belief things can change for the better. Muna's life experiences, the shaping of a character, the finding of a vocation. Is her choice of work linked to her experience of FGM?

'For sure! For sure!' Muna does not hesitate.

It is her outspoken campaigning against female genital mutilation that pushed her towards where she is now, pushed her to become the most influential voluntary activist in Somalia.

Before Mogadishu, in Beledweyne, Muna began a campaign against FGM. She criticised the practice on television and on radio, on social media, at podiums, in newspapers, in blogs. She became a force to reckon with, a strong woman deserving attention.

'FGM needs to stop,' she told her listeners.

Al-Shabaab was in the audience. 'Insulting Islam' is how it described Muna's anti-FGM campaign, and so she started receiving death threats: 'Watch out! We are coming for you.' Al-Shabaab brings to a violent end the lives of those who 'mock Islam'.

'I did not stop for nothing. I continued what I was doing.'

But she could not knowingly endanger children. She could not live in the village anymore. She fled to the safety of Mogadishu's chaos.

Al-Shabaab, or 'the youth', is a militant organisation that seeks to establish a Sharia-based Islamic state in

Somalia that would ultimately encompass the Horn of Africa. Formed in the late nineties, al-Shabaab enforces an ideology that supports the killing of unbelievers. Their troops, reported to be well over twelve thousand strong, regularly stone, amputate and behead criminals and apostates, violently prosecute non-Muslims and clash with humanitarian workers.

Al-Shabaab is responsible for ninety per cent of the violence in Somalia. Muna takes on al-Shabaab on a daily basis.

'I facilitate workshops and other meetings between youth and influential people – clerics, celebrities – who can motivate them towards a meaningful life,' Muna explains.

'Most of al-Shabaab fighters are youth and eighty per cent of Somalia's population are youth.'

Muna as an influential youth leader and al-Shabaab as an armed recruiter of youth are working – with vastly different purposes – towards the same goal: attract the mind and touch the heart of the disaffected and the disillusioned young adult, the angry young men and women of Somalia hurtling aimlessly through their short, brutal lives. Al-Shabaab takes advantage, recruiting them into their army, turning them into killers, perpetrators of violence – relentless, merciless violence, in the name of a most merciful God.

Muna's work is to persuade the same youth otherwise. She meets with them in prison, in youth camps, in schools, in refugee camps, in the inner city. They are everywhere.

'There is almost eighty per cent unemployment. Can you imagine what this means? They have nothing to do.'

The number of orphans increases in parallel with the high death toll. Many children grow up under care, in theory. In practice, they remain uncared for. Rich pickings for al-Shabaab.

'I am raising this issue again and again. The youth need to be a part of the country's development. They need to feel ownership of it,' Muna says.

Experts on 'radicalisation' agree that counter-narratives, which provide alternative views to those expressed by organisations like al-Shabaab, can help reduce the chances of these organisations succeeding in seducing young minds.

'The Qur'an is best for counter-narratives,' Muna says. 'When you can show young people – using the Qur'an – that al-Shabaab is manipulating them, and manipulating Islam too, it is easier to draw them away from dogma.'

As a layperson without a scholarly background in Islamic education, how is she able to facilitate such workshops? How is it allowed?

'If you have the clerics with you, it is possible.'

Even for a woman?

'Yes.' Muna has the backing of clerics, who often appear at her workshops for young people.

What drives ordinary people to commit acts of 'Islamic terrorism' is not Islamic teachings but ignorance of them, says the heavy literature.

'When there are young people looking for solutions, adventures and answers, and al-Shabaab is using Islam to recruit them into war,' Muna says, 'we provide them with the strength and the knowledge – drawn from the Qur'an – to resist.'

Muna Hassan, supplier of mental ammunition to resist the call to arms. Word before sword.

'Change how people think, that's what we have to do.' I have heard her say this before.

Is there a more mammoth task a person can take on than causing a paradigm shift in a society's way of thinking about and acting upon something? The degree of difficulty multiplies when arms, bombs and brute force are held up in resistance to the intended changes. Like al-Shabaab's resistance to the changes Muna wants in people's thinking: the emancipation of women, saving girls from the razor, boys from the gun, adults from forced submission to the will of another.

Muna and al-Shabaab in direct opposition to each other.

Life is short; particularly if you are a Somalian living in Somalia. A female Somalian human rights activist living in Mogadishu, who advocates for gender equality, denounces as a violation of human rights the revered ritual of cutting girls, meets with political leaders to tell them exactly why they are wrong, uses the Qur'an as her weapon of choice against religious militants killing in the name of Islam – Muna, why are you risking your life so?

'I need to live in peace. I need my people, my family, to have peace. If I do not take risks, who will? As long as I am taking risks, my children, the younger generation can survive.'

I want to phone Muna again for an update on the meeting with the Prime Minister. And to hear her voice – how can it be light, coming from a place of such darkness? Muna faces the worst of human behaviour with its best. She is certain a better world is possible.

'I am in Kenya,' a fertile al-Shabaab recruiting ground.

I will call another time.

Muna is busy.

LINA BEN MHENNI (Tunisia)

written by Laura Cassidy

In 2007, at the age of twenty-four, Lina Ben Mhenni started writing a blog. In the same year, at the age of twenty, I started writing a novel. That decision has given me many incredible opportunities, the most unexpected being the chance to correspond with Lina, and learn more about her life and activism.

Lina called her blog *A Tunisian Girl,* and wrote posts in Arabic, English and French. 'I started it by sheer coincidence,' she tells me. 'I wanted to share texts that I was writing. I was not expecting to experience what I am living today. In the beginning, I just wanted to express myself in a country where it was impossible to do so.'

Lina wrote about human rights violations and censorship under the rule of the former Tunisian president Zine El Abidine Ben Ali, and was one of only a few bloggers to use her real name. Her site was blocked in Tunisia, and her computer seized. But she continued to document the injustices she witnessed, including police violence against protestors. Her blog and others like it played an important part in the revolution that brought down Ben Ali's twenty-three-year dictatorship.

Now thirty-five, Lina is still blogging. An award-winning activist and journalist, she has been nominated for the Nobel Peace Prize and invited to speak at events worldwide. Her decision to blog in three languages was initially an organic one. 'Usually I don't choose the language I am writing in. When I start writing, words come on their own in a certain language. But during the twenty-nine days that led to the departure of the dictator Ben Ali, I published each blog post in two or three languages to reach a larger audience around the world. It was the first time that I had decided to make a linguistic choice.'

Lina grew up in a family of activists. Her father, Sadok, was a political prisoner, and her mother, Emna, was part of the student union movement. Lina was aware of their work from an early age. 'As soon as I started to understand language, I became aware of my parent's activism. I could hear words like "prison", "politics", "comrade". I saw these comrades come to our home and heard their discussions. My father was one of the founding members of the Tunisian branch of Amnesty International, and some of their meetings took place at our home. I listened to those conversations with great curiosity. Later, I discovered the presence of books with jail stamps in our library, and started to ask questions, wanting to understand.'

Her father went on hunger strike in prison for the right to read, and would later pass on his love of books to Lina. 'Since I was in my mother's womb, my father was reading me books,' she says. 'When I opened my eyes, a library was waiting for me.' Lina visited prisons through her activism, and was concerned by the reading materials she saw on the shelves of prison libraries, many of which were fundamentalist in nature. In response, Lina and her father set up the 'Books to Prisons' scheme. Their call for donations went viral, and they've since gifted over thirty thousand books to prisons. When I ask Lina to pick three of her favourite books to include, she struggles to narrow them down. 'It is really hard to answer this question. It is really difficult, there are so many interesting books.' Eventually she settles on *The Unbearable Lightness of Being* by Milan Kundera, *The Forty Rules of Love* by Elif Shafak and a book by one of her father's comrades, Fethi Bel Hadj Yahya, entitled *El habs kadhab wel hay yrawah*. 'The title is a Tunisian idiom meaning: even if you are in prison, you should keep the faith and be hopeful you will be released.'

Lina's own freedom has been compromised by her activism. It has led to personal threats, and the need for twenty-four-hour protection from the police. But she doesn't doubt her path. 'I have never regretted becoming a human rights activist. It is true that my situation today is really annoying and tiring, but I believe in what I am doing. I am doing it out of passion, love and conviction. I cannot stop doing it. It is true that the price to pay for that is very high. When I first heard about the threats targeting me, I thought that it was something temporary. I still remember the day a group of policemen knocked on my parent's house and informed me that they were my new security group. I could not accept it that easily and met with the Minister of Interior, who showed me proof of the fact that I was targeted by religious extremists. I had to adapt to this new situation. I always fought for my freedom and that of others and I lost mine on the way. But I don't regret it, I love what I do.'

In the beginning, Lina's parents were dubious. 'They were frightened by the long hours I was spending typing in front of my screen. They believed that I had abandoned my books and studies. They believed I was playing.' But they soon realised the importance of her blog, and encouraged her. 'They only asked me to be careful, as my health is delicate.' Lina was diagnosed with lupus as a child and received a kidney transplant the year she started blogging. She was prevented from exposing her body to the sun because of her illness, and instead tattooed a sun on her back. The star tattoo on her left hand also holds significance. 'It is the star from the Tunisian flag. If one day I feel that the main objectives of the revolution are fulfilled, I will draw the crescent too.'

In some ways, a typical day in Lina's life doesn't sound that unusual. 'The first thing I do after I wake up is have a look at my emails, my Facebook account, Twitter and Instagram. I do that wherever I am. If I am home, I get ready, prepare my coffee, and feed my cats. After that, I plan my day, depending on my meetings and commitments; sometimes I have conferences, meetings, interviews. Before leaving, I always have to make sure that I am carrying my camera and laptop with me. There are always unexpected events to report. I also have to call my guards. If I do not have events or activities, I clean my house and read or write. At other times, I wake up elsewhere, in another country where I am invited for a conference or a congress.'

Lina is vocal about women's rights in Tunisia, and has experienced the challenges faced by many opinionated women on the Internet. 'As a blogger and activist I am all the time targeted by defamation and insulting campaigns. But people do not discuss or criticise my ideas. They are attacking me based on my gender, my clothes, my look. With male bloggers, it is different.'

Social media was instrumental in bringing about the Tunisian revolution, and I ask if Lina is concerned about its negative aspects. 'Social media allows us to network, to know new people all over the world. It facilitates exchanges and makes things easier. It is true that some people are using social media to spread hatred, but the amount of people and organisations using it to do good is important. Social media helps in giving voices to voiceless people. The free access facilitates things. I will say that it is a double-edged sword and the results depend on the way it is used. It is just a tool and its impact depends on us.'

Lina is very active on social media, while my participation is more sporadic. But during our two years of correspondence I check her pages regularly, to see how she is doing. One afternoon, not long after cutting my hair short, I click on Lina's Facebook page to find her long hair gone too, replaced with a pixie cut almost identical to mine.

After watching hours of impressive online footage of Lina's speeches and interviews, I wonder how she feels about public speaking – if, like me, she ever experienced a reluctance. 'To be honest, I do not like to speak in public,' she says. 'It makes me nervous and I start shaking whenever I am on stage. I am an introverted person and prefer to express myself through written texts. But I feel that I have a responsibility to interact with people and to share my experience with them. After each speech I am usually surprised by the audience's reactions. People come up to see me and express their gratitude, to say that they liked my speech, and to ask questions.'

Amazingly, I get the opportunity to witness this in person when I meet Lina during the Dublin Human Rights Festival. We see each other for the first time on a November afternoon in the banquet hall of the Smock Alley Theatre, minutes before we are interviewed for a festival event. In person, Lina is strikingly petite, passionate and articulate. After the interview, in which we talk about our experiences of the project and Lina's activism, we make our way through Dublin with the project organiser, Orla, stopping for Lina to take photos of the Christmas lights glinting above the crowds of shoppers. I look at the streets I've been hurrying through with fresh eyes, and feel a swell of my limitless love for the city. At the packed festival after-party we listen to music and spoken word in a room that pulses with talent, energy and optimism.

Lina is keen to explain why she hasn't been as active in her work recently; she's been unwell, and hospitalised due to her lupus. But I point out that even while in hospital, she continued to help people. From her bed she set up a donation programme that aims to give Tunisians easier access to life-saving medication.

With regard to Tunisia, Lina feels that there is still much work to be done. 'From the outside, the Tunisian revolution is seen as a successful one. But when people took to the streets and faced real bullets and tear gas, they were mainly asking for jobs, freedom, and social justice. When I look at the situation now, almost none of these objectives were achieved. Politicians seem indifferent to the needs of young people and seem to nurture corruption, injustice and inequity.'

I ask if she will continue to blog until she feels the objectives of the revolution have been achieved, until she can finally add the crescent to her hand. 'Blogging has to do with writing and I think that we cannot stop writing. When Ben Ali fled the country I told myself: He is gone, what am I going to write about? A few days later, I understood that there are always causes to fight for. When you choose to use your pen or laptop to help others, to give a voice to voiceless people, you do not stop. It is an everyday fight.'

FRAGMENTS OF A LIFE (Tunisia)

written by **Lina Ben Mhenni**,

translated by **Dr Míde Ní Shúilleabháin**

Fragment one: death by life

The realisation comes at an early age that dying begins at the moment of birth. Comprehending our mortality is one thing; however, it's quite another to live with the constant, immediate and very real threat of death. A death that lurks inside us, crouched in the darkest corners of our being, in the depths of our genetic make-up, a terrible beast waiting for our physical defences to weaken, waiting for the right moment to strike at our vital organs. Or a death that will come in the sting of a bullet or with the flash of the blade brandished by a killer for hire, who emerges from behind a palm tree or at a bend in the street, proclaiming God's name and moving with the terrible confidence of his absolute impunity. Or a death by public servant, as an agent of the state, a supposed protector, brings his heavy-duty boot down – as if by accident, but with such hostility! – on the exact part of your body he knows to be the most vulnerable. I have been living in the shadow of all these possible deaths for twenty-five long years.

I was only eleven years old when the sun and the sea and so many other things I loved dearly were first taken from me. In their place came the agonies of countless medical treatments, rendering my days long and grey. And so I learned to control my spirit in order to survive. The more I suffered, through kidney failure, dialysis and transplant, through the side effects and consequences of these, the better I became at exercising this control.

During the years of my illness, I lost a close family friend, a man who had been like a second father to me. For a number of days following his death, I was left without the power of speech. His was not the only passing; during this time, I lost others very dear to me and with each loss came a greater understanding of what it means to die.

My many hospital stays brought other encounters with death; one of which was at the bedside of a neighbouring patient, who I helped in her final moments. Death became increasingly anchored in my psyche as a result of these experiences, with the result that for a period of several weeks I refused to be treated in hospital, leading to the rejection of my transplant and to the start of my lupus (disseminated erythematous).

Then, one day in February 2011, as the whole world celebrated our revolution, I nearly died of asphyxia on the city centre's Revolution Avenue, crushed under the weight of a dozen henchman who, angered by the photos I was taking, were determined to seize my camera.

There were countless times before and after when I was subject to, or sometimes narrowly escaped, beatings, abuse and assault. Were it not for the support of my parents, brother and fellow demonstrators, I would not be in a position to tell my story today.

The attacks did not end with the revolution. On the evening of Saturday, 31 August 2014, as I travelled to Jerba – that happy island of my parents, that mythical island where Ulysses was bewitched by sirens and lotus-eaters – a policeman who had been assigned to my protection led me into a custom-designed trap. The heavy boots that rained blows upon my body that evening seemed especially drawn to the exact area of my kidney transplant. I really don't know that I would have made it through had others not raised heaven and earth to have me released.

I was, indeed, the 'beneficiary' of a personal protection service – an armed policeman, whose presence had been imposed on me by the Minister of the Interior himself. The Minister justified this by the fact that I was the target of death threats, some of which had been passed on to me via media sources. These death threats linger and continue to be issued to this day.

I live under the constant threat of death, resisting the illness that eats away at me from the very depths of my being, and ignoring the Damoclean sword that any number of government thugs or violent reactionaries could at any time cause to fall on my neck.

Staring down danger. Confronting my lupus. Facing up to my transplant. Never bowing before any type of terrorism. Combatting impunity. Putting my own struggles to one side to better lend myself to the struggles of others. Never wavering in the belief that life deserves to be lived but never forgetting, either, that to live is to live well, to live generously, to live is to resist. This I learned from my daily encounters with death.

Knowing this has empowered me to keep living. And I will keep living, and living fully. And as for you, my lupus! And you, my kidney! As for you, forces of evil, you terrorists, torturers, persecutors! I defy you and I rejoice in the defiance. Because I have beaten you before and I will never give up.

Fragment Two
As I became increasingly familiar with life's dark twists, I developed revulsion for the police; for all members of the police. This revulsion more than likely first arose when I caught my first glimpses of the scars that my father bore not only on his body but also on his soul. Scars that he tried so hard to hide from me but of which I first learned – at least as I recall it now – from snooping through papers that I was never meant to read and from catching snippets of discussions that I was never meant to hear.

Revulsion. Not hate.

There were, however, occasions – rare occasions, perhaps, but occasions all the same – when I allowed myself to be overcome by feelings of hatred towards members of the police and even towards the police as a whole. One such instance was on 9 April 2012, when the uniformed thugs of the new regime tried to stop us from taking our protests up Revolution Avenue. My father, while trying to protect me, was slapped and thrown to the ground by a government goon young enough to be his grandchild.

I experienced this same feeling of hatred on another occasion when Omar, a follower of one of the city's football teams, was given a 'swimming lesson' in the muddy water of the waste treatment centre. And then again one evening in Regueb, when, after taking a photo of his prone body, I bent down to kiss the forehead of [name omitted], shot down only a short distance from his parents' home and was struck by his radiant smile, by his expression of absolute release.

There were other times, too, it cannot be denied, when I succumbed to feelings of hatred. Times that I prefer not to recall; however, I can honestly say that I never gave in to hate when I myself was attacked by government henchmen. Neither before 14 January 2011 nor directly afterwards, in that period when many possible futures still existed for the country. Nor in those months and years that followed when our country was plunged once again into disillusion and despair.

This I swear, and I swear it proudly.

I still experience a feeling of revulsion towards the police. But this revulsion never turns to hatred. Never.

I did not give in to hatred on those many occasions when I was attacked. Nor those many times when I was threatened. Not even when one of the dictator's lead flunkies, in the days leading up to the January 2011 revolution, practically called for me to be eliminated by showing my photo and publicly broadcasting my name. And not when a so-called man of God did the very same during a television broadcast in 2012.

Hatred did not win out when my protectors turned into predators and left me for dead. Nor when, accusing us of having attacked them first, a group from Jerba went after my parents and me.

No, even though the feeling of revulsion remains strong today, I have never allowed hatred to take over. So, yes, the revulsion is still there but every day it transforms a little more into pity. I often feel pity for my persecutors. I feel sorry for them. Sometimes I even feel shame for them. But that never turns to hatred. Sometimes I am filled with rage at them. But this is a rage that never turns to hatred.

I have been able to preserve my inner calm despite all the attacks to which I have been subjected. When the Minister for the Interior imposed a personal protection service on me, thus bringing me into close contact with several agents of the state, this allowed me to develop a degree of perspective. Knowing that there were martyrs in the ranks of the state's various armed bodies has brought home to me that – as the saying goes – 'the web of our life is of a mingled yarn, good and ill together'.

And so it is that good judgement has become my guiding principle.

Fragment Three

Good judgement, you say?!

Yes. Good judgement. Through the attacks. The broken spirits. The betrayals. The tight corners. The support offered from unlikely sources. The support withdrawn where it had been counted upon. The anonymous tip-offs and warnings. The averted gazes and sudden desertion of those you thought would always be there for you. The strangers coming unhesitatingly, courageously, wholeheartedly to your aid. The friends who turn from you and who divert their path from yours when they sense the unrelenting presence of danger that surrounds you, or when they realise how financially hard up you now are.

The policeman who, recognising you at a traffic stop, can't stop apologising and swears to you with tears in his eyes that not all cops are bastards. The elderly lady who insists on getting a photo with you and whispers the proud promise that her first granddaughter will be named after you. The sneering Facebook message – 'Out to get the Nobel Peace Prize, are you?' – of a lowlife lackey of the new regime. The bellowing policeman who aims his tear-gas canisters at you, declaring that nothing would give him more satisfaction than to smash your skull into a thousand pieces.

The prison guard in a high security jail who falls sobbing into your arms, who tells you that the very fact of your being is a comfort to her, who says that in you she sees a friend, a sister, a mother, a saviour, and who declares in front of her colleagues that she is ashamed of her profession. The seasoned informer, whose services are always available to the highest bidder, who sends you messages full of lies and calumny and calls you a sell-out, a flunky. The respected elder who goes to great lengths to try to recruit you as a founding member of his new party.

The strangers who establish a committee for your defence, who support you through illness and danger, who light up your parents' house with music and candles. The asshole of a self-styled Salafist 'emir' who stops you from entering the town of El Omrane in Menzel Bouzaiene and tries to block your support for the region's hunger strikers. Your father whose few well-chosen words have such force that they strip the charlatan of his pretensions and send him packing. The duplicitous pretenders and the leeches disguised as friends and revolutionaries. The very real protection of those gentlemanly guardian angels who make you feel like you are so much more than a security assignment, who treat you like a sister.

Black is black; white is white.

What crap! That's not how life is.

The good judgement that has come with life lived under constant threat has taught me to see the world in many shades.

Fragment Four

Good judgement, calmness, reason, objectivity, magnanimity, generosity, forgiveness.

But also: anger, rage, suffering, pain, despair.

To see our unexpected revolution – with its winds of change that opened so many doors and gave freedom to so many diverse thoughts and opinions – trampled upon, falling to its enemies, self-destructing, sliding ever further backwards: it hurts. It hurts immeasurably with a pain that eats away at calm and undermines good judgement.

These young men and women who dared to dare, who showed that the impossible was indeed possible, who invented a new type of revolution, who took us by the hand and led us, from the caves in which we had been huddled, down the path of freedom and towards the realisation that our one true destiny was simply to be human, that our one true destiny was to support the peoples of the world in experiencing the struggles and joys of citizenship; to see them stumble even as they took their first steps; to see how quickly they have forgotten their martyrs, have forgotten the sacrifices of blood and sweat, forgotten even those longed-for horizons that once they strived towards; to see them fractured, lost, turning their backs on the dream that once drove them, instead chasing after the mirages of material comfort – to see this is to be seized with rage, to be filled with a bitter anger at the emptiness and resignation that now reign.

To see one's country spiral downward when once it had been heading towards a beautiful future; to see the older generation – those responsible for making our todays so dark and dull – snatch from the youth those rays of colour and sunlight that they had discovered; to see how self-proclaimed defenders of the faith have persecuted women and womankind; to see how violence and assassination are committed with both arrogance and impunity – this is enough to wear one down to the point of being overcome by anger and rage, to the point where surrender can seem like the attractive option.

Anger at the hold you have on us! Anger at ourselves. Anger at others. Anger at individuals, at the collective. Anger at life. Devastating anger. Overwhelming rage.

Despair.

Fragment Five

One day when I was overcome by the effects of tear gas (imported from Brazil, let me remind you), a protestor who had rushed in to drag me out of the way of the batons being wielded dangerously close by, found nothing better to say by way of encouragement than, 'You're young, with the strength and health of youth, so get up, ignore the pain and start walking. Otherwise you're done for, and me along with you.'

What choice did I have other than to do as I was told?

When I think back on that incident, I realise that my entire life has been an episode of getting-on-with-it, of running and outrunning as if I were endowed with the lungs of an Olympian. My life has been committed to living fully – to living normally and to living at full speed.

Determination. Obstinacy. Stubbornness. Tenacity. Perseverance.

The truth is, I never had a choice. Even with death lying in wait in the deepest cells of my body, even when the threat of death hung over me daily, I never stopped believing that I was born to *live*. To live fully.

Life has become the one song that I sing, my one reason for being; life is more than something that I desire – it has become a delight, a permanent rainbow of joy and challenge as well as an almost unwitting gift in itself.

When one loves life, when one is determined to live life to its fullest, determined to experience fully every second of every day, when one has learnt to look towards the positive, life becomes ever more beautiful, more precious, more appealing.

Life transforms into a warm protecting embrace that envelops you in comfort and happiness. As the shadows fade away, hope is born anew and bright perspectives emerge and entice.

There's not a word of exaggeration here. I'm simply sharing a bit of my life, fragments of who I am. Loving life with all that I am has taught me how to love others, all others, in their differences, contradictions and diversity.

Having loved and not knowing how to do other than to continue to love, I have come to believe deeply that my life is lived in the lives of others. By this, countless paths have opened for me and by this too my fight for my own life has become a fight for life itself.

For those seeking to walk down this path with me or to fight other good fights, some words of advice: Eradicate torture. Revive memory and seek out sites of conscience: prisons, labour camps, sites of summary executions. Be a voice for those who have no voice. Be Tunisian: champion local business. Fight impunity. Support the families of the martyrs and casualties of the revolution. Be inventive in ensuring those in need have access to treatment and medicine. Promote collective and individual freedoms. Denounce all ill treatment, including mistreatment of our friends in the animal world.

If we love life, the threat of death should not stop us from taking action and from living better lives.

T (Sudan)

written by **Hilary Fannin**

I took the train to meet T, travelling past suburban back gardens and beyond the damp city centre to where the built landscape falls away and there is nothing to see but sea. I know the shape of the coastline around Dublin Bay intimately; this city has been my home for more than half a century. Sometimes its familiarity sticks in my craw and, like the seagulls overhead, I want to screech and reel.

Walking through the urban village where we have arranged to meet, it occurs to me that I shouldn't arrive empty-handed. I stop at a bakery, buy cakes, pass the time of day: *oh the rain, the rain, the rain, tsk tsk tsk.* We all know the drill.

The cakes sit untouched on the table between us. T is cold, doesn't take off her coat. She has a lovely face, soft, pensive, terribly young. She holds her hands together in her lap.

'I am thirty years old,' she tells me.

I have no idea how to begin to unravel T's story. I roll out some bluster about the rain, but she is weary of the Irish weather and I am speaking too fast and I know that she has to work hard to understand and communicate in English. And I know, too, that mock-despair about a damp morning is indicative of belonging; it points to the luxury of inclusion. And this country is not T's home, and home is where she wants to be.

I look beyond her composure and I see something else: sorrow.

T's home is Al-Fashir, the capital city of North Darfur. Darfur is a region in western Sudan with a population of seven million in an area roughly the size of Spain. In 2003, when T was a teenager, war erupted in Darfur when rebel groups began fighting the Sudanese government, demanding greater political and economic rights for communities in the region. That war would become the first genocide of the twenty-first century, with hundreds of thousands of civilians dying from violence, disease and starvation, and more than two million men, women and children being displaced from their homes.

The first genocide of the twenty-first century. 'Genocide' – it's a word heard on the radio, on the television news, not something most of us can envisage experiencing.

In Dublin in 2003, in those febrile days of the booming new millennium, I found myself living in suburbia with two young sons. While the radio belted out advertisements for four-wheel drives, I'd tempt my two-year-old into his buggy so that we could walk down to the school to collect his older brother. Closing the door on the lunchtime radio news, we'd leave behind the voices of journalists and aid workers describing the mass slaughter and rape of men, women and children in western Sudan, their reports punctuated by ad breaks rhapsodising over ever-so-meaty cat food.

I remember during those long, domesticated days becoming aware of the name Janjaweed and vaguely understanding that it referred to some kind of a militia, men who travelled on horseback. I didn't know, or want to know, that the Janjaweed were armed and supported by the government of Sudan in their mission to systematically destroy Darfurian villages, burning homes and crops, looting businesses, polluting water, murdering, raping and torturing entire communities.

I didn't then, and still don't, have a language for that level of atrocity, for the relentless despair it brings with it. I'd watch my young sons run around under a big grey sky on this damp island and try not to think about what the word 'genocide' actually meant. 'Genocide', noun: the deliberate and systematic extermination of a national, racial, political or cultural group.

Now, more than fifteen years after that conflict began, T and I sit at a table in the Dublin offices of Front Line Defenders, in a room that has been vacated for us. Outside, telephones ring, conversations echo; there is a sense of urgency, of camaraderie. I try to remember what I have hastily taught myself about Sudan, the country of T's birth.

Bordering the Red Sea, Sudan, at the start of the conflict in Darfur and prior to 2011 when South Sudan seceded, was the largest country in Africa. It is a police state. President Omar al-Bashir has led a hard-line administration since coming to power in an Islamist-backed coup in 1989, when sharia law was implemented.

Someone brings us tea. The cakes, I am told, won't go to waste.

I have never been to Africa. I have spoken to people who have lived and worked in Sudan and have been told that Sudanese society is complex, layered, a place of hostile social attitudes but incredibly warm people. I have been told that sharia law doesn't apply to non-Muslims in the country.

Sudan's capital, Khartoum, where T went to university, is a city, I understand, with a well-educated, thriving middle class. Anecdotally, I am told of a Khartoum elite who shop in New York and bank in Geneva. It's difficult to conflate this information with what I have read about human rights abuses in Sudan.

Among these violations, there are innumerable examples of violence against women. I am reminded in my reading of the social media outcry in 2010 when a video went online showing a Sudanese woman screaming as she was whipped for wearing trousers. I have been reading, too, about the relatively newly constituted 'No To Women's Oppression' group in Sudan, who are using social media to highlight the countless incidences of women who are arrested and flogged each year for wearing the wrong clothes or simply for being out with men.

Illustrating the complexity of the society, I have learned, too, from people who work in the country, of numerous influential Sudanese women employed in medicine, teaching and technology and of the decision-making power they have in the workplace.

T is a human rights lawyer. Her work in North Darfur was to represent women and girls who had been subjected to sexual violence there. At the time of our meeting, she had been in Ireland for six months, having been brought to Dublin by Front Line Defenders for respite, a service the organisation offers to human rights defenders who are dealing with extreme stress.

I quickly realise that T does not feel safe speaking too specifically about her jobs both with a private law firm dealing with humanitarian cases and with the Sudan Social Development Organisation (SUDO), a human rights and international development body working with displaced persons and civilians affected by conflicts. T still has colleagues working in the office from which four policemen took her, put her into a car and drove her away to a detention centre outside her town. I sense that she is acutely fearful, even now, of saying something that might put the liberty of those former colleagues at risk.

I don't know how much T will be prepared or able to talk about her arrest, imprisonment and subsequent flight from her home place because of the work she was doing. I tell her that I am just a conduit, a pen, a keyboard; I am at her disposal to tell as much of her story as she wishes to share. I claim to understand her fears, but I am lying. I understand nothing of T's world.

We begin by speaking about T's life growing up in Darfur, and about her family, of whom she is immensely proud. 'All my family are activists, bringing awareness,' she says.

T's mother was a teacher, who died when T was a child. Her father, who still lives in the region, is a health activist, his job is to teach people about disease eradication and caring for their environment. After the death of T's mother, her father remarried, but his second wife, who took care of the family, also died at a young age.

T tells me that her father, despite the trauma of losing two wives, was utterly committed to the education of his children, both boys and girls. Now adult, T's brothers and sisters work mostly in the area of healthcare. Her eldest brother is a health activist, another brother qualified as a doctor, while her two sisters, whom she misses greatly, are a nutritionist and an officer in a UN agency. She also has a younger brother who is an engineer and another who works in information technology.

After T's release from prison she lived for a brief period in Egypt, where she was able to receive visits from some of her family, including her father and his new wife. However, when a warrant for her rearrest was issued in Egypt through the Sudanese embassy, she had to leave that country too. She is extremely grateful to her family members for all the support they gave her at this time.

She has not seen her family since 2017. Now living and studying in a British city, she doesn't know when, or indeed if, she will be able to return home. Not long ago, her sister, who still lives in Al-Fashir, opened the door to a policeman wanting to know about T's whereabouts.

I ask T for a memory from her childhood and she tells me how, after the death of her mother and before that of her stepmother, many homes in Al-Fashir, including her own, were destroyed by rain. The loss to her family was great, as theirs was a 'healthy house', with sanitation. After the first house was destroyed, her father tried to build another, but it, too, was destroyed by rain; all the rooms flooded, schoolbooks and uniforms destroyed.

Amid the chaos, there was looting, and people tried to steal their things – the TV, the fridge, the family's clothes and possessions.

All this took place at a time of immense difficulty in her community, T explains. It was a time when the city was crowded with the dispossessed and many, many people were without homes.

I ask what happened to T's mother.

'She was ill for a long time. She had rheumatism. She travelled to have care in the capital city, and she died there.'

I'm trying to understand the psychological impact on T of losing her mother, her stepmother, and her home. When I ask her how it felt to be a child growing up in these tumultuous circumstances, she brings me back to the importance of her education, reminding me of her privilege and telling me that she was one of the lucky ones.

I ask her if education is free in Sudan. She smiles. Education is supposed to free, she tells me, it is written into the constitution of the country. Sadly, however, the reality is different. She tells me about overcrowding in Darfur's schools and about areas of western Sudan where there is little or no access to education. 'Also, we have a big problem for girls. Some areas have stopped educating them.'

'Why?'

'To marry.'

'To marry at a young age?'

'Yes. A lot of groups do that.'

T went to a mixed secondary school with girls and boys. Then, in 2004, her father left his government job and, a year after the start of the conflict, began working in the camps in North Darfur. It was through her father's work that T first experienced the scale of need there.

Aware of her educational advantages, T worked hard. Her father wanted her to study medicine; her passion, though, was law and history. Determined to help the people of Darfur and refugees fleeing over the border from Chad and other countries, she finally chose to study for a law degree.

'What was your day-to-day life like when you were going to school in Al-Fashir?' I ask. 'Were you secure? Were you safe?'

'In my city, the afternoon and mornings were safe,' she tells me. 'But at night it is very dangerous because maybe someone will pull out a knife and take your money. In 2008, me and my sister, I think about eight in the evening, we were walking to the shop at night and someone took her mobile phone and her money. But at night thieves can also come into your home. But outside of the city, in the villages, it is much worse. Morning or afternoon, houses are entered and women raped and killed. But inside the city it is just dangerous at night.'

'And so people left their villages to come to the city?'

'Yes, at the start of the conflict they left their village just to search for safety, because all civilians became victims.'

In 2015, T's father was nominated to stand for election as a member of parliament while T, then in her late twenties and working as a human rights lawyer, was helping to organise protests against the election because of corrupt registration procedures that resulted in many civilians being unable to vote.

'Did your father respect what you were doing?' I ask.

'Yes, yes. Our family, uncles and aunts, couldn't understand this, but he understood my opinion and said to me, "All right, this is your opinion."'

'He seems like a unique man.'

'Yes. Our community is closed-minded; it is difficult for girls or women to speak about free ideas. Also, in our [extended] family, some elders, they didn't want me to continue my work to protect women and girls from harassment in taking rape cases. But I studied law because I know the Darfur area. I understand how Darfur people suffer. I wanted to do something useful for them. I had a teacher in university, also a Darfurian, who taught us [about] human rights. He could relate to and connect with our situation in Darfur and in all of Sudan.'

T later tells me that human rights was not taught officially at her university in Khartoum and that when, back in university in Al-Fashir, she planned to write about humanitarian crimes for her master's degree, the university bench refused, telling her that she couldn't do that as she would have no valid reference point to base her thesis on. She tried to argue her case by saying that she had plenty of material to draw on, but she was still refused.

T finally qualified with a master's degree in peace and development studies from Al-Fashir University and a bachelor's degree in law from Khartoum University. By this stage, her ambitions had crystallised: she wanted to work to obtain justice for women and children who had been raped and abused by the government militia.

T and I have by now been talking for some time. She looks drawn, cold. Outside, the Irish weather is doing what the Irish weather does, spitting out rain and thinking about thunder. I am worried about continuing our conversation, but she wants to keep talking.

I want to ask her about fear. I am aware that in parts of Sudan sexual violence and intimidation are widely understood to be used to silence female activists. I want to try and understand why T elected to do the work she did when she could, with her education, have chosen, like her siblings, a different profession and a quieter, more secure life.

T seems to disregard the question about why she chose to be a human rights lawyer, though her reasoning will surface later. She tells me that in all areas of work for women in Darfur, communities can be closed-minded. 'Sometimes it's tough for women even to study for a master's.'

As for the work of female activists, she explains that yes, it is difficult to travel to other villages because of the documentation the police insist on and also because of the danger of violation. T's relatives, she says, often advised her not to visit the camps around Darfur to take statements from women and girls who were raped, because of the danger that T herself could face. 'Often there is no security or police around these areas,' she says.

T goes on to tells me that many marriages of female lawyers, friends of hers, have ended in divorce because a woman can find herself working long hours. (I find myself thinking that forfeiting a husband would probably be the least of my worries if I were a female human rights lawyer in western Sudan – but this is no laughing matter.)

T takes time to think about her response to my initial question about why she chooses to do the work she does.

'In Sudan, a lot of people have the courage to do something,' she says. 'They have power and skills to do something, but still they are afraid.'

I take it from that response that T herself is not afraid.

She tells me a story about an incident that she and a female colleague were involved in shortly before her arrest.

During the Sudanese general election of 2015 – the one in which T's father sought office and which was won by the incumbent president, Omar al-Bashir, after the majority of the opposition boycotted the ballot – she and a female colleague were defending four students who had been arrested for demonstrating against the debilitating cost of education. The students had been taken into police custody, and when T and her colleague arrived to see their clients, the police officer in the station physically attacked T and tried, more than once, to hit her.

A relative of one of the students intervened, while her colleague tried to photograph the incident. Another policeman then arrested her colleague and put her in an isolated room, where he beat her.

The women, when they finally got away, wrote a complaint against the policemen, which they presented to the bar association. However, on returning to work, T discovered that the policeman who'd tried to assault her had made a complaint against her, claiming that she'd hit him. The police had, in fact, filed six separate criminal complaints against her.

The case was finally dropped due to lack of evidence, but by then T's name was on file and she had become much more vulnerable to future harassment by the police. Advised to keep a low profile for a period of time, T stopped work for about three months and went to Egypt, where she began to write a book documenting some of the cases she'd been involved with.

I ask T whether this current essay and interview could be used as a vehicle for her own words to find an audience? I feel, as we speak, acutely aware of my lack of detailed understanding of her world and work. I'm aware, too, of her belief that if she can tell the stories of the women and girls she has represented, the world will listen.

I'm not so sure. I think about, but don't share with her, my own sense of being overwhelmed by stories of brutality and inhumanity. I don't know how to have a coherent response to all the information about war and famine, terror and mania, that rolls across our screens, deafening us, sometimes ultimately cauterising our sympathy. The sheer scale of injustices in the world can disable our ability to react. And then I try to imagine how T, sitting here in her coat, fragile yet determinedly lucid, must feel, telling her story to another stranger in another country, a country doused in rain and preoccupied with its own domestic crises.

T wants lawyers and activists in Sudan to read her book. She has, however, stopped trying to publish it, because of the potential danger to colleagues and family and to the victims of rape and sexual assault she has spoken to for her research. The book enumerates the many ways women are prevented from reporting crimes against them and the difficulties they experience in bringing rape charges. She speaks about the reasons that crimes go unreported in Sudan, and it all feels deadeningly familiar: the lack of facilities to take medical evidence; the way women are treated when making complaints, which can feel like another assault; the amount of evidence that is lost; the cases that are dropped due to lack of evidence; the often terribly young age of the victims.

At the time of T's arrest, she was handling almost fifty rape cases; most of these, she explains, were hampered by lack of physical evidence. T tells me that there is a three-day window to collect evidence of rape, but with no hospitals and few police stations, this was often an impossible time limit. Added to this, she says, is a lack of awareness in some communities of how to deal with rape victims. Some people wash away evidence without understanding the implications, others are coerced into washing it away.

'Case after hard case,' T says quietly, 'case after hard case.'

Often unable to travel to outlying villages herself, due to the nature of her work and the danger she might face from the police authorities, she sometimes has to rely on her paralegal colleagues to gather evidence from victims, including copies of medical reports if they exist.

She shares with me some of the reports that she tried but was unable to bring to court. They make grim reading.

'Would you like me to include these cases in our essay?' I ask her on the phone. She says that she would, and sends me the details:

> (R) was raped by three criminals (M, N & A) in Shangil Tobaya village in 2/1/2016. She was eighteen years old when she was raped. The accusal was opened in Shangil Tobaya police office and was referred to Al-Fashir Court, but the criminals denied the charge and the victim was accused of fornication, because there was no evidence or medical report. The lawyer stopped the procedure to protect the victim (R) from the crime of fornication because she would have been punished in accordance with the Sudanese Criminal Act 1991.

> (F) was fifteen years old when she was raped by a soldier (H) in Alkokola village. The accusal was opened in Kutum police office, where he was arrested. A military group followed the accused to the police office and removed him with weapon force. The procedure was dropped.

> (F) was seventeen years old when she was raped by three military on 18/6/2016. The soldiers' names were unknown. The accusal was opened in the children protection police office in Al-Fashir. The file with the medical report was hidden by police. The lawyer didn't find the official file of the accusal. She had an official copy of the medical report, but the police refused to use the copy to continue the proceedings. The police order a new medical check and report on the 26/6/2018. All medical evidence gone.

(A & K) were twelve and fourteen when they were raped by unknown military on 11/1/2015 in Kungara village. The accusal was dropped in Al-Fashir because it was recorded as an unknown criminal case.

(H & S) were raped in Tabet on 18/5/2018. They recorded their data in the military office but not to police because they didn't find police in their area. Accusal dropped.

(M, S & K) were raped by a military group in Tawilla on 24/4/2015. The case was recorded in a police office but it was dropped because of lack of evidence.

*

T was arrested on 26 December 2016, bundled into a car by four police officers and driven to a detention centre outside her town, where she was interrogated and told that her crime was political. She had been arrested, she was told, because she insisted on saying that there were a lot of rape cases in Darfur even though the government of Omar al-Bashir said there was no rape in Sudan.

T's arrest followed that of a close colleague whose computer was confiscated by the police and whose emails were examined. I ask her if she suspected that her arrest was imminent once the confiscation had happened?

'Yes, and I was afraid that they would arrest me and ask me about my email, because I have a lot of information. But when I was arrested and [the police officer] asked me about my password, I gave him the wrong one.'

At a human rights centre in Sudan, T and her colleagues had received some training in case of arrest, so when the police arrived at T's office, she was able to jettison her mobile phone with all the details of her contacts. She also quickly hid paperwork and gave her briefcase, with the notes it contained, to a male colleague.

'In Sudan, a lot of activists (and also one journalist) are raped when they are arrested, and at first I think maybe I will be raped in prison, because there are cases like this,' she says. 'But I had training about how to deal with this. When I was arrested, my colleague stayed with me until I was taken away.'

'Was he with you for long?' I ask.

'No, just for the first few minutes until I was taken away. We had two minutes of eye contact.' After T had been brought from the detention centre to another unknown police station, her possessions were taken from her and, handcuffed, she was put into another police car with four more officers and driven to the airport.

On the plane to Khartoum, T recognised two human rights activists who, having been released from custody in Al-Fashir, were being returned to the Sudanese capital. T managed to sit behind the activists and when she was briefly left alone by one of the four guards who accompanied her on the flight, she wrote her father's telephone number on a piece of tissue and handed it to one of the freed activists.

After T had been arrested, messages had also been relayed to her uncle, and money was made available for her father to travel to Khartoum, where his daughter, after her terrifying ordeal, was now on remand and being held in isolation in a women's prison.

'Did you see anyone?' I ask. 'Did you know what was happening to you? Did you have any books or were you able to write?'

'I did not know what was happening to me or for how long I would be in custody. I only ever saw the female warden who brought me food. After some days, they brought me books, but only specific types of books about Islam.'

'Were you afraid?'

'Yes. When I was in the police station there were a lot of men. I was afraid because I know what happens. I know it's easy to commit security violation in Sudan. But afterwards, when I was in the women's prison, it was okay. But I didn't know how or if I could go outside.'

T's father arrived in Khartoum on the day after she was imprisoned there. He waited for twenty-three days before he was allowed a single visit to his daughter. Then, on the fifty-fourth day of her incarceration, T was taken to court for a judicial review. There she was told by the judge that she would be released if she would swear to return to court and give evidence against her boss at the private law firm she worked for in Al-Fashir, a man she greatly respected, who had dedicated himself to dealing almost exclusively with humanitarian and rape cases.

After much deliberation and conversations with her father, T agreed to this ruling and was released. Her father was there to take her home. T, however, never had any intention of returning to court to testify against her colleague. After much soul-searching, T persuaded her father to allow her to escape to Egypt. Reluctantly, he agreed. The price T would pay for her loyalty and integrity would be the loss of her family and of her country.

T ultimately spent three months in prison in Sudan and a further three months in Egypt, teaching a little but moving every month in order to avoid the warrant that had been issued for her arrest through the Sudanese embassy in Cairo. Finally, exhausted and dispirited, and having managed to make a short visit back to Sudan to see her family, T realised that she was unsafe in Egypt. Were she to be arrested again, she could spend years in prison, deeply vulnerable and with no visitation rights.

It was at this point that she made contact with Front Line Defenders and a visa was obtained for her to come to Ireland. And so she was introduced to the rain, and to further uncertainty, and to a cloudy, lonely kind of freedom. She is, she says, enormously grateful for her safety. She has had to leave behind her two great loves, her work and the family whose support has sustained her throughout her years fighting to give a voice to those women and girls who so often remain unheard.

'And so here we are.'

'Yes.'

Our tea is cold. Beyond the long windows, the shape of Dublin Bay is just visible. I watch the gulls reel – mocking, ceaseless, endlessly in pursuit of the next crust or beak-full of entrails, the next fleeting satisfaction.

'How do you see your future?' I ask. 'If you could wave a magic wand, where would you want to be? What kind of life would you want to have?'

'I prefer …' She hesitates. 'My colleagues say it's better if I stay in a country where I can practise my English, because I want to study more. But Egypt is better for me, to maybe see my family.'

'And beyond that?'

'In the future?'

'Yes.'

'I don't know. I want to stop my work. I want to make a family. I want to stay in one place. Maybe I can study, because to marry and study in one place is easy.'

'You would like to marry and study and have a family, all in one place.'

'Yes.'

'Have you met anyone you'd like to marry?'

'No. Maybe in future.'

'Well, you never know what is around the corner.' She laughs. I find it hard to join in.

'A lot of men in Sudan have a closed mind,' she says, as if reading my mind.

'You said something a few minutes ago that kind of stopped me in my tracks,' I tell her. 'You said your work is your duty, that if somebody needs your help, it is your duty to help them.' I flip back through my notes. 'You said: "I will die, at some point I will die, but this work is my duty. I need to do this work." Is that correct? Have I got that right? "I will die, at some point I will die, but this work is my duty. I need to do this work."'

T looks at me levelly.

*

When we next speak, on the telephone, T has moved to Britain. A refugee, she cannot return to her country and her future is still not clear. She plans, she tells me, to go back to her country when the Sudanese government falls. (There have been reports in recent weeks of unprecedented numbers of women taking to the streets to join the daily nationwide protests that first erupted in mid-December 2018. Despite a violent crackdown by the security forces and reports of sexual harassment, the protesters, of whom women make up at least seventy per cent, have remained defiant in the face of the repressive laws of the state.)

T has obtained a place at a college, where she now studies business and IT. She has sounded bright and happy in our recent communications. She is volunteering with a charity and has found friends and camaraderie with the Sudanese community of the city she now lives in. Just last week she was given the keys to her own flat and was able to move out of the hostel she had been living in.

'How's the weather been?' I ask.

'Bitter.'

'Bitter?'

'No. Better.'

'Better is better than bitter.'

'Yes, it is.'

To begin to understand T is to begin to understand something about courage. Despite so many odds, her need for anonymity, her struggle to communicate a complex story through English, her sadness, her displacement, her loss of home and family, all the fear and trauma and isolation she has lived with, her concerns remain with those she has left behind, the women and children whose cases remain unheard, unresolved. T is at pains to point out to me in every interaction we have that systematic rape crimes have continued in Darfur since the beginning of the armed conflict in 2003 and that the Sudanese government has failed to recognise or act on many of these crimes.

I had been clear with T that this essay was *our* essay, authored, in so far as possible, by both of us. I had asked her for a section of her book to include, and she chose the following. It is indicative of her solidarity and support for those subjected to brutality and a testament to her faith that, by documenting these stories, hope can be maintained of obtaining justice in an unknown future.

> Most of the rape cases in Darfur took place in circumstances where victims and civil and humanitarian organisations, who have been trying to fight for rights and punish criminals, have suffered from legal and natural obstacles and lack of access to justice. Under Sudanese law, in some cases this has led to victims being considered criminal and to the escape of rapists from justice. These circumstances have been exploited by the Sudanese government to hide crimes against humanity in Darfur.

T goes on to provide an example:

> (H) was raped by two soldiers on 18 June 2016, when she was seventeen years old. She and her friend had gone to collect water at a water source more than five miles outside her village when the two girls were attacked by two men on motorbikes, wearing military uniforms and carrying weapons. Her friend escaped. (H) was kidnapped by the two men, who took her further away from the village and into a mountainous area free of people. There they both raped her. No one could hear her, she couldn't return to her home from the side of that mountain, she was far from home and there was no transport in those small villages.

> It was noon when her friend returned to her village. Nobody knew where (H) was. A search was initiated by villagers and (H) was found around 8 p.m. in the place where the crime had been committed.

> There was no clinic for medical examination, no emergency hospital, no laboratory; there was no police station to go to for an immediate medical report, no one to write a legal report. On the second day after she was discovered on the mountainside, her family travelled with her to Al-Fashir.

There they had a medical report done and also made a legal report in the police office dealing with child protection. A police officer took the original medical report and told the family that there were no more procedures to follow. Four days later, the family met with a legal aid lawyer. She went to follow-up proceedings with the family and child protection police office. There the policeman looked for the original medical report; however, he had not recorded the date on which the medical report was issued. Neither was there any information about the crime in the police files. The policeman recommended to the lawyer that she instruct the family to get a new medical report and make a new complaint. At that stage, the medical evidence had been removed from the victim's body.

This case contains all the factors that contribute to the concealment of rape crimes in Darfur.

1. The exploitation of systematic military force, which weakens the resistance of the victim to the criminals.

2. Exploitation of power, demonstrated in the bringing of victims to places from which they cannot easily escape. In this case, the victim was brought to the side of the mountain. In other cases, victims have been taken to cliffs.

3. Lack of medical, legal and transportation services in Darfur. In the villages, there are no hospitals or health centres where first aid would be available and medical evidence taken. Transportation between the villages and cities is hampered by the lack of proper roads. Few villages have police stations, so some of the victims resort to complaints to non-police military bodies.

4. Exploitation of victims' lack of legal awareness. Complaints are recorded in the wrong way. Original medical documents are taken and hidden without registration, making it necessary to obtain new medical reports, after the disappearance of medical evidence. This changes the nature of the crime and turns rape into adultery. After a long period, the data of the medical report is often changed, in order to turn the rape crime into adultery.

5. Exploitation of weak legal and health work. Doctors are often unable to prove the legal issue of rape crime. There is a lack of diligence within the police, which leads to regular failure to build a case against and arrest criminals. The Sudanese government has exploited these kinds of situations and has hidden crimes of rape committed in Darfur by removing all evidences of such crimes.

Sixteen years after the conflict began and the UN Secretary-General's most recent report to the Security Council on the situation in Darfur asserts that it remains relatively stable except for intermittent clashes between government forces and the Sudan Liberation Army. The report states that while there is a decrease in human rights incidents, attacks against civilians, particularly internally displaced persons, have continued with impunity, and sexual and gender-based violence remains a serious concern.

*

It is late evening, and T and I are speaking on the phone. T is not going to give up; her commitment to the fight for justice seems immeasurable. I wish her luck in her new home, and she thanks me. Her excitement at finally having a place to call home is clear.

Home.

I ask T if there is anything else she would finally like me to add to our essay, and her response is swift. Yes, she says, she wants me to make it utterly clear that mass rape by the military is continuing in Darfur. She goes on to tell me the names of eight women and girls who were raped in Darfur on two dates in February and March of 2019. 'It is important, Hilary, that we don't forget them, but you must not use their names as we are trying to bring them justice.'

I read the names of the eight women and girls to myself, their sound and rhythm so unlike the names I am familiar with: Jayne and Rosie, Una and Geraldine, Mary and Louise, Karen and Anna. I'd like to write down their names so that you could hear them for yourselves, could imagine that name being called out by a sister or friend. Their enforced anonymity feels like a further crime against them.

Where were you on 5 February 2019, when five women were raped by the military in Umhashaba village when they went out to collect firewood? I had an appointment in my gym that day, to have my programme altered, as some of my weights were too difficult to manage.

Where were you on 9 March 2019, when three women and girls were raped by the military in Dala? (One of them – let's call her Anna – was fourteen years old. According to available reports, she was also tortured.)

I was a bit tired on 9 March. It was a Saturday. I'd had a busy week. I'd been reviewing a show and I had a newspaper column to write about a book launch I'd attended. The following day, I was due to travel to Belfast to see some theatre produced by young writers.

The plays were impressive. One in particular stood out, a sort of love story written by a young writer of fourteen. I watched her come onto the stage to take her bow, fourteen years old, full of hope and joy, her whole beautiful creative life ahead of her.

Postscript

In mid-April 2019, as I was preparing to submit this essay, Omar al-Bashir was toppled by the army after thirty years in power. At the time of writing, a military council has pledged elections in two years' time. Protesters remain camped outside army HQ in the capital, Khartoum, demanding a civilian administration. I find myself tempted to imagine that T's dreams of returning to her home, her work and her family might just be within sight.

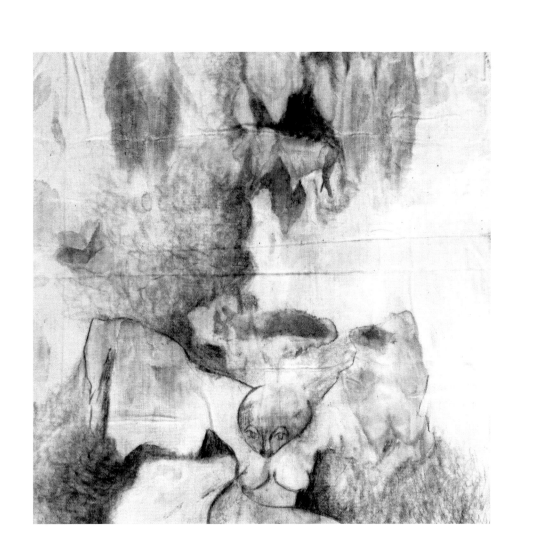

CONTRIBUTORS

NURCAN BAYSAL is a Kurdish human rights defender and journalist from Diyarbakır, south-eastern Turkey. Her work documenting human rights violations committed by Turkish forces in the region has garnered strong condemnation from nationalists and pro-government groups and individuals. In January 2018, she was detained and charged in connection with her tweets calling for peace and condemning the Turkish government's military incursion in Afrin. In February 2019, she was acquitted of this crime. In February 2018, in a separate case, she was sentenced to ten months in jail for allegedly demeaning the Turkish security forces in a 2016 article about war crimes committed by in the Kurdish town of Cizre.

LINA BEN MHENNI is a Tunisian woman human rights defender and blogger, who played an active role in the 2011 revolution. As well as campaigning against social problems, she advocates for human rights, particularly freedom of speech, women's rights and students' rights. Through her blog and social media accounts, which were censored under the Ben Ali regime, she documents protests throughout Tunisia. Lina was the recipient of the *El Mundo* International Journalism prize and the Deutsche Welle International Blog Award in 2011, and the Sean MacBride Peace Prize in 2012.

HADEEL BUQRAIS is a woman human rights defender and writer. She works freelance to monitor and document human rights violations by the Kuwaiti government. Previously, she worked for Kuwait Watch, an NGO that works on the development of legal protections for people in Kuwait, and is the founder of a human rights school. She has been actively involved in a campaign called Namshi Laha, calling for gender equality in Saudi Arabia, as well as a campaign called Ringing the Bell, which seeks gender equality in Kuwait.

LAURA CASSIDY is a writer from Co. Kildare. Her first two novels, for young adults, were published by Puffin Ireland. She is a recipient of the Cecil Day Lewis Literary Bursary Award and is represented by the Darley Anderson Agency. Laura is a founding editor of the literary journal *Banshee*.

ROSA DEVINE is from Dublin, Ireland and has worked as a graphic designer, illustrator and educator. She has published comics with *Sliced Quarterly*, *Vast Expanse*, *Sunday Comix* and *The Irish Times*, and was a contributing artist to *Draw The Line*, which won the 2017 Broken Frontier Award for Best Webcomic.

Photo by Refik Tekin

ZEHRA DOĞAN is a Kurdish artist, writer and journalist from Turkey. She is a founding member of JINHA, the first all-woman, feminist news agency of Turkey, which was closed by an emergency decree in 2016. Zehra was arrested in July 2016 on charges of membership of a terrorist organisation for her articles and paintings illustrating the curfews and operations in Kurdish towns. Released at her first trial, she then was sentenced to thirty-three months and imprisoned in June 2017. She continued painting in prison, using whatever she could find as paint – herbs, fruits, and even blood. She was released in February 2019. Zehra is the recipient of many awards; most recently, she received the 2019 Index on Censorship's Freedom of Expression Award in the art category.

CATHERINE DUNNE is the author of ten published novels. Her one work of non-fiction, *An Unconsidered People*, is a social history that explores the lives of Irish immigrants in London in the 1950s. Among her novels are: *The Things We Know Now*, which won the Giovanni Boccaccio International Prize for Fiction in 2013 and was shortlisted for Novel of the Year at the Irish Book Awards, and *The Years That Followed*, which was published in 2016 and was longlisted for the International Dublin Literary Award. She is the recipient of the 2018 Irish PEN Award for Contribution to Irish Literature.

EZRENA MARWAN is a Malaysian graphic designer specialising in identity, web and print design. She draws on archival practices and graphic design theory to examine the intersection of visuality, history and politics, with a particular focus on issues of identity, violence and power embedded within visual culture. Ezrena uses her work to focus on those who are normally marginalised by design. Her portfolio is thick with work created in support of social and rights-based organisations and initiatives around the developing world. Ezrena is an archivist and one of the founding members of Malaysia Design Archive, a platform that aims to give context to the history of graphic design in Malaysia.

HILARY FANNIN worked as an actor throughout the 1980s and 1990s. Her first play was staged in London in the mid-1990s. Her writing since then includes numerous stage and radio plays. Hilary was joint writer-in-association at the Abbey Theatre for its centenary year, 2004. She is co-creator and mentor of a playwriting course for teenage writers run by Fighting Words in association with the Abbey Theatre. Her memoir, *Hopscotch*, was published by Doubleday in 2015. Hilary began writing for *The Irish Times* in 2004 and currently writes a weekly personal column for the paper. A recent graduate of the MPhil in creative writing at Trinity College Dublin, her first novel will be published by Penguin Ireland in 2020.

NIAMH FLANAGAN graduated from fine art print at the National College of Art and Design, and is now a member of Graphic Studio Dublin, where she also works as projects manager and master printer. Selected solo and group exhibitions include: *Dwellings of Mind and Space* (2007), The Printmakers Gallery Dublin; *Île d'Hiver | Winter Island* (2009), Centre Culturel Irlandais, Paris; *Artist's Proof* (2009), Chester Beatty Library Dublin; *An Elsewhere Place* (2012), Graphic Studio Gallery Dublin; *From Islands to other Seas* (2016), Graphic Studio Dublin; *Inside Worlds* (2017), SO Fine Art Dublin; *Collision* (2017), the Law Society of Ireland and 188th RHA Annual Exhibition, Dublin. Her work is in the collections of the Office of Public Works, the Law Society of Ireland, the British Library and the National Gallery of Ireland.

MUNA HASSAN MOHAMED is a trade unionist, social activist and woman human rights defender. She has worked in leadership positions in youth-led civil society organisations such as Somali Youth Cluster, Hiiraan Youth Organisation, Coalition for Grassroots Women Organisation and Somali Peace Line. She was a leading member of the National Disaster Response Volunteers that came together to assist relief and rescue operations immediately after Somalia's worst ever terrorist attack, in October 2018, in which over three hundred civilians were killed and hundreds more seriously injured.

ORLA LEHANE is Education Director at Fighting Words. She has a background in arts and human rights education, having previously worked with Front Line Defenders and Amnesty International.

Photo by Ashley Miller

MONICA MCINERNEY is the Australian-born Dublin-based author of twelve bestselling novels and a collection of short stories, published internationally and in translation in more than twelve languages. Her newspaper articles have appeared worldwide in *The Guardian*, *The Sydney Morning Herald* and *The Australian*, among others. She is a member of Irish Pen, the Australian Society of Authors and a volunteer at Fighting Words in Dublin.

Photo by Simon Robinson

LIA MILLS writes novels, short stories, essays and an occasional blog. Her most recent novel, *Fallen*, was the 2016 Dublin/Belfast Two Cities One Book festival selection. She has been an invited contributor to anthologies of stories and essays such as *The Long Gaze Back* (edited by Sinéad Gleeson) and *Beyond the Centre: Writers on Writing* (edited by Declan Meade). Her work has appeared in, among others, *The Dublin Review*, *The Stinging Fly*, *The Irish Times* and *The Dublin Review of Books*. She is a founding member of the Freedom to Write Campaign (Ireland), a group of professional writers who work informally with human rights and literary organisations to promote freedom of expression.

AZRA NASEEM studied journalism in Ireland and worked as a reporter in Dublin for several years. Originally from the Maldives, she writes about human rights abuses and social issues in her country, focusing especially on religious extremism and its effects on communities.

SHEILA O'FLANAGAN is the award-winning international bestselling author of more than twenty novels and three collections of short stories for adults, as well as two novels for children and young adults. Her work has been translated into over twenty languages.

MELATU UCHE OKORIE was born in Enugu, Nigeria. She has an MPhil in creative writing from Trinity College Dublin. Her work has been published in *Dublin: Ten Journeys One Destination*, *Alms on the Highway* (New Writing from the Oscar Wilde Centre), *LIT Journal*, and *College Green Magazine*. Her debut collection, *This Hostel Life*, was published in May 2018. She is currently working on a novel.

SEHAM OSMAN is a woman human rights defender, Nubian minority activist, and founding member of Genoubia Hora, the first feminist group in Aswan, southern Egypt. She founded the organisation in 2012 in response to what women human rights defenders have called a 'widespread acceptance' of both police violence and violence against women. She was a leading member of, and one of the most visible women in, the Nubian Caravan, a protest movement campaigning for the rights of the Nubian indigenous peoples to return to their land.

LANA RAMADAN is a woman human rights defender, who was born in Dheisheh refugee camp, near Bethlehem in the West Bank. Previously, she has worked with Badil Refugee Resource Centre as a researcher focusing on forced displacement and coercive environments created by Israeli policy. Since December 2017, she has been working as the international advocacy officer at Addameer Prisoner Support and Human Rights Organisation, a Palestinian non-governmental organisation supporting Palestinian political prisoners held in Israeli and Palestinian prisons.

T is a human rights lawyer in Sudan, who provides legal assistance to victims of human rights abuses.